PARENTING
MADE
SIMPLE

Dr Sarah Hughes is a respected clinical psychologist, author and media commentator. With over a decade's worth of clinical experience, she's an authority on everything from toddler tantrums and teenage drama, to body image, work–life balance and relationships — parenting, personal and professional.

Dr Hughes is best known for her work with teenage girls, in women's mental health, and her straightforward, practical — and real — parenting advice. Her relatable, down-to-earth style has seen her become a regular commentator on television, radio and print media.

Dr Hughes completed her clinical training at the University of Sydney and holds a Doctorate in Clinical Psychology and a PhD in child and adolescent anxiety disorders. She founded Think Clinical Psychologists, the team private practice she works from, in 2011, and lives in Sydney with her un-husband Shane, son Harrison, and dog Max.

Sarah loves helping parents to navigate the rabbit warren that is parenting. If you have feedback, parenting questions or stories you'd like to share, connect with Sarah via her social media (DrSarahHughes) or the 'Ask Sarah' page of her website (www.drsarahhughes.com).

PARENTING
MADE
SIMPLE

STRAIGHTFORWARD, PRACTICAL
STRATEGIES FOR COMMON
CHILDHOOD CHALLENGES

DR SARAH HUGHES

EXISLE
PUBLISHING

First published 2020

Exisle Publishing Pty Ltd
PO Box 864, Chatswood, NSW 2057, Australia
226 High Street, Dunedin, 9016, New Zealand
www.exislepublishing.com

A CiP record for this book is available from the National Library of Australia.

ISBN 978 1 925820 32 4

Designed by Enni Tuomisalo
Typeset in EB Garamond, 11.5pt
Printed in China

This book uses paper sourced under ISO 14001 guidelines from well-managed forests and other controlled sources.

10 9 8 7 6 5 4 3 2 1

Disclaimer
This book is a general guide only and should never be a substitute for the skill, knowledge and experience of a qualified medical professional dealing with the facts, circumstances and symptoms of a particular case. The information presented in this book is based on the research, training and professional experience of the author, and is true and complete to the best of their knowledge. However, this book is intended only as an informative guide; it is not intended to replace or countermand the advice given by the reader's personal physician. Because each person and situation is unique, the author and the publisher urge the reader to check with a qualified healthcare professional before using any procedure where there is a question as to its appropriateness. The author, publisher and their distributors are not responsible for any adverse effects or consequences resulting from the use of the information in this book. It is the responsibility of the reader to consult a physician or other qualified healthcare professional regarding their personal care. The intent of the information provided is to be helpful; however, there is no guarantee of results associated with the information provided.

For Shane, my parenting partner in crime, and Harrison, who loves us despite our many parenting 'fails'.

CONTENTS

INTRODUCTION

Have kids, they said. It'll be great, they said. And it is — most of the time. But it's not all great. Parenting is bloody hard work. It's all day, every day, 365 days a year. There's no HR department to step in when things turn sour, and no employee entitlements like paid holiday leave, sick leave or overtime for those long sleepless nights. And those are just the standard, run-of-the-mill parenting challenges all parents face. If you have a child who tantrums at the drop of a hat, a child who's highly sensitive and clingy, or a child whose inability to make friends and paralysing self-doubt keeps you up at night, parenting is an even harder task.

Every child comes with their own unique set of parenting challenges, but there are also common challenges nearly all parents face. Challenging behaviour, emotional outbursts, friendship problems and confidence issues are usually part of that mix, and with divorce and mental health statistics being what they are, parenting anxious kids and parenting the 'right way' through separation and divorce are challenges testing parents these days as well. Arming yourself with the right strategies is key, and the good news is you don't have to sort through hundreds of parenting books to figure it all out. The strategies you need are covered for you right here in this book.

If your child's behaviour is driving you up the wall and you're feeling in over your head, breathe. There's a lot you can do to turn things around; you just need the right strategies, and to know when and how to use them. The chapters in this book have you covered. And if your child's pretty well behaved, but you'd like straightforward, practical parenting advice — not vague, general advice that leaves you no closer to understanding exactly what it is you need to do — on how to raise a calm, confident, well-adjusted and resilient child, keep reading. What you need to do *and* how you need to do it, is covered here in detail, and it's easier than you might think.

And if you need help but you're insanely busy and don't have time to read this book cover to cover, don't stress. Each chapter is self-contained and addresses a separate childhood challenge, complete with hypothetical case examples based on the hundreds of families I've worked with over my years in private practice. You don't have to read the book in full to find the parenting answers you need, just the sections you need help with now.

Grab a coffee, and let's get started.

1

WHEN YOUR CHILD'S BEHAVIOUR IS TESTING YOUR PATIENCE

There are hundreds of reasons why being a parent is hard, but challenging behaviour would have to be pretty high on the list. It leaves most parents, even highly skilled ones, feeling exasperated and more than a little on edge. There's the toddler tantrums of the terrible twos (which, let's face it, start earlier and last longer than that) and beyond that, as your child gets older, other challenges creep in as well — a sassy attitude, backchat, power struggles over homework just to name a few.

When your child's behaviour shifts from compliant to challenging, you'll question your capabilities as a parent and start to worry that all your worst fears have been realized and you're raising a delinquent. But the truth is, *all* children go through periods of poor behaviour, even kids with terrific parents. If it feels like everyone except you has delightfully well-behaved children, rest assured, the parents you're comparing yourself to are either keeping the worst of it under wraps or their time is yet to come, and they'll feel the full force of the teenage years in the not-too-distant future. No parent is lucky enough to avoid misbehaviour all together, I guarantee it.

Your child's behaviour won't be this challenging forever, but there's next to no chance of them undertaking a massive behavioural overhaul of their own volition. Change needs to be led by you, and there's a lot you can do to teach your child to behave well, but the trick is this: strategy choice. Behaviour management isn't a one-size-fits-all game. If the strategies you use don't address the underlying causes of your child's behaviour, it doesn't matter how well you implement them or how consistent you are in your approach; your efforts won't translate into behavioural change. To successfully change your child's behaviour, you have to hand-pick the right strategies and, to do that, you have to understand how things got so off-track in the first place.

Common reasons kids misbehave

Maybe they express their dislike for the word 'no' through monumental tantrums, use physical aggression to tell you what they want and when, or have a habit of developing a temporary hearing problem when asked to do something they don't want to do. If your child's behaviour is testing your patience, it's easy to fall into the trap of thinking they're deliberately acting up just to push your buttons. But there's usually more to it than that. In general, kids misbehave for one of two main reasons: either they lack the skills they need to behave well, or they've been taught to misbehave (albeit completely unknowingly) by their parents.

Common parenting behaviours that contribute to misbehaviour are listed below. Use this information to help you explore your own role in your child's misbehaviour and, before you dismiss this as a possibility, remember all parents — even parenting 'experts', myself included — fall victim to these traps every now and then.

You don't give me attention otherwise

Kids love feeling like they're the centre of your world. When it comes to learning and behaviour, whether the attention on offer is positive or negative is irrelevant; any attention is reinforcing.

It might seem backwards, but if your child's behaviour is being driven by a need for attention, even long drawn-out admonishments can end up encouraging the behaviour you don't want to see. It's why time out can be so hit and miss as a strategy. If your child willingly stays in their time out area for the duration of their time out, it can be effective. But if you have to chase them around the house to keep them there, the extra attention only serves to encourage a repeat performance.

Attention is a powerful reinforcer. Take note of which behaviours are grabbing yours most.

You're expecting too much of me

Misbehaviour can be the result of expecting too much too soon. If your child doesn't have the cognitive skills needed to process multiple instructions such as 'I want you to get dressed, pack your toys away, and take your dirty dishes to the sink', this will be a hard ask. Likewise, if your child's still learning to resist distractions, the chance of them getting themselves ready for school without at least a few prompts along the way is slim. You might want your child to be ready for more but your expectations need to take your child's developmental level into account.

Expecting too much too soon will lead to frustration for you and your child. Make sure your expectations are realistic.

You keep changing the rules

When it comes to learning, consistency is key. If the rules keep changing, your child doesn't know what you want. Think back to when you taught your child how to identify shapes. Each time you saw a square, you pointed to it and called it a square. When you saw a circle, you told your child 'circle' — and with repetition, your child learnt what those words meant. If you sometimes labelled a square a square, and sometimes called it a circle, though, confusion would slow your child's learning. Learning rules for behaviour is no different. If your child receives different feedback on different days, or if one parent enforces rules and the other doesn't, it's confusing.

Kids learn through repetition and consistent feedback. An inconsistent approach, no matter what your child's age, will lead to misbehaviour.

You don't always follow through

All kids test limits. It's not a sign your child's a delinquent — even though it might sometimes feel that way. It's a sign your child has a healthy curiosity about how the world works. How you respond to limit testing is what's important. Hearing you talk about consequences is one thing, but seeing you follow through is another. When you don't follow through, you as good as teach your child that you don't mean what you say, and that's a dangerous message to impart when behaviour is an issue.

You haven't told me what I should do instead

When kids misbehave it's easy to fall into the trap of giving one-sided feedback, but for kids to behave well they need to know what you *want* them to do, not just what you want them to *stop* doing. The right course of action might seem obvious to you, but unless you teach your child how they can achieve their end goal without misbehaving, their misbehaviour will continue.

You don't give me a chance to feel in control

There's a lot kids aren't in control of. They're told what to wear, when to eat, what they can and can't do and when — in a sense, they're micromanaged. As parents, we know there's good reason for this, but kids don't see things the same way. From a young age, it's normal and healthy for kids to want to feel they have some control over their lives. When they're not given this opportunity, they rebel. They test boundaries and act out, all in the name of asserting their independence. Helping your child to feel like they have some control is a common, and effective, fix for misbehaviour.

I'm hungry/tired/not feeling well

When kids are hungry, tired or not feeling well, they find it harder to regulate their behaviour. It might seem like an excuse, but think about how you react when you're sick, tired or hungry. As adults, we're more prone to irritability and emotional outbursts when we're tired, hungry or sick, and kids are no different.

You've taught me that misbehaviour works

Consider this: you're on the phone and your little one's tugging at your shirt because he wants to speak to you. You're trying to focus on your conversation so you ignore him, but his tugging gets more and more insistent and so does his whinging. You eventually break — '*What*?!? What is it? What do you want? Yes, you can have another cookie!' Bingo. Yes, he knows you're mad because your tone has made that clear, but his joy at getting what he wants will overshadow this. In fact, you've taught him — without meaning to — that if he persists and is annoying enough, he'll get what he wants, and that's a lesson he'll use to guide his future behaviour as well.

Because you do it

Kids are pretty observant, and more often than not they're most observant when we don't want them to be. They learn a lot from what you do, not just what you say. You might tell your child to speak nicely and not yell at others, but if he sees *you* calling someone a bad name or overhears you mouthing off, he'll do the same thing. When it comes to your child's behaviour, it pays to remember that your actions are just as important, and sometimes even more important than your words. You need to teach your child to behave well by leading by example.

How you respond to your child's misbehaviour is important. Respond in the 'right' way and misbehaviour will be short-lived, but inadvertently respond in the wrong way and the likelihood of that behaviour reoccurring is increased, tenfold.

But as important as your responses are, they're not the only factor at play. Your child's behaviour is also being affected by their developing cognitive skills. Let's take a closer look at how that side of things works.

Behaviour + the developing brain: why kids *can't* always behave well

Good behaviour is more of a skill than you might think. To behave well, kids need to be able to remember rules, manage their emotions, think flexibly, and inhibit impulses. For littlies in particular, there's a lot to learn. If kids don't have the skills they need to behave well, it won't matter what rewards and consequences are in play, misbehaviour will continue, because challenging behaviour isn't a choice, it's the result of lagging skills. And before you think I'm giving your child a get-out-of-jail free card, science backs this up. A growing body of research supports the idea that kids misbehave because they don't yet have all the cognitive skills they need to behave well. Why? Because their young brains are still developing.

Your child's brain will undergo huge change in the first five years of life. More than a million new neural connections will be formed every second — a rate of growth that won't be replicated at any other time over the course of your child's development. And it's these connections that will change and shape your child's cognitive, emotional and behavioural skills.

We know from research that different parts of the brain develop at different rates. Areas of the brain that support more basic functions like vision and hearing develop first, followed by areas that support early language skills, and then higher-level cognitive functions. One of the most important areas of the brain still undergoing development throughout childhood and adolescence is the prefrontal cortex. The prefrontal cortex has various functions, but one of its most important is supporting a group of cognitive skills known as executive functions. Executive function skills include skills for planning, time management and organization, skills that support our ability to pay attention and inhibit impulses, and skills for flexible thinking and emotional control — basically, all the skills kids need to behave well and meet our expectations.

By adulthood, our executive function skills can be broken down into three key skills: working memory (the ability to temporarily store information and then use it in some way), cognitive flexibility (the ability to flexibly switch from one activity to another), and inhibitory control (the ability to ignore distractions and resist temptation). Research in preschoolers, though, seems to suggest that in children, executive function is an undifferentiated, unitary construct, and that it remains undifferentiated until at least seven years of age.[1,2] In fact, some research suggests that individual skills (working memory, cognitive flexibility, inhibitory control) continue to change and develop at different rates well into early adolescence.[3]

What this means is that in children under seven at least, executive function skills are still at a relatively basic level. Why is this important? Because if executive function skills are still developing in childhood, then so too are the skills that support positive behaviour.

Good behaviour is learnt

Your child is still developing the cognitive skills they need to think flexibly, control their attention and manage their emotions. They're also still learning how to integrate these skills to regulate their behaviour. Repeat performances of challenging behaviour might make it seem as if misbehaviour is deliberate, but odds are your child *wants* to behave well but lacks the necessary cognitive skills they need to please you — and that's where you come in.

There's a lot you can do to help your child learn how to better regulate their behaviour, but it's going to mean changing your mindset when it comes to behaviour management. The key message is this: good behaviour is learnt. You need to *teach* your child how to behave well, through skills training and the lessons you instill through your parenting.

Choosing the right strategies

To change your child's behaviour, you need to understand *why* they're misbehaving. Skip this step and the strategies you use may not be the right ones, and your efforts will be wasted. If you have no clue why your child's misbehaving, monitoring will give you a better idea of what factors might be at play. It's hard when you're juggling work, family and life in general, but pick a week, and over the course of that week pay attention to your child's behaviour, close enough that you can gather intel to answer the following questions. Your answers will help guide your strategy selection.

- What happened to trigger my child's misbehaviour? Had they been given an instruction? What activity were they participating in? Could what happened before the misbehaviour be a clue to what's driving it?

- What feeling might have precipitated my child's misbehaviour? Is it possible their behaviour is a symptom of not knowing how to manage frustration?

- When my child misbehaved, what happened next? How did I respond? Could my reaction be inadvertently reinforcing my child's behaviour, either through attention-based reinforcement or modelling?

- Is there a common thread to my child's misbehaviour? Is there a lagging skill that might account for most variations of misbehaviour?

- Does my child have a clear understanding of what's expected? Have I explained what I expect and backed this up consistently in my parenting?

Once you have a better understanding of why your child's misbehaving, you can look at which strategies will work best. A number of effective behaviour management strategies are outlined below. Look at what's causing your child's misbehaviour and match this to the strategies.

If you glance over these strategies and think, 'I've tried this before and it didn't work', read the information carefully and double and triple check that you've been executing the strategy correctly, which includes making sure you've been adapting strategies properly for your child's age and developmental level. Strategies only work if they're executed correctly, and small errors can make a huge difference to a strategy's effectiveness. Rewards charts are a great example. A lot of parents are sceptical when I suggest we try one. They tell me they've tried rewards in the past and they've never worked, but that's because they haven't implemented them correctly. Their tune quickly changes once they're in the habit of using rewards the right way.

If you're not sure how to adapt strategies for your child's age, you'll find specific guidelines in the section below. These guidelines will help you better understand how to adapt strategies for littlies (three- and four-year-old children), younger children (five- to ten-year-old children), and older children (eleven and twelve years). Keep in mind, these are rough guidelines only — make judgments on adaptations based on your expert knowledge of your child.

Set clear expectations

When you're trying to address problem behaviour, the first thing you need to do is set clear expectations. Pitch your explanation to your child's age, but when you're explaining what you want your child to work on, be specific. General language like 'be good' makes it hard for your child to know exactly what you want them to do. Use specific language, like 'keep your hands and feet to yourself' (an appropriate goal for littlies or younger children) or 'listen and do tasks when asked' (appropriate for older children) and explain clearly what you want your child to do. If the behaviour you're targeting is 'good listening', for example, explain what this means by saying something like, 'Good listening means listening to what Mum and Dad ask you to do. So if we ask you to come to the dinner table and you stop what you're doing to come as we've asked, that would be good listening. If we have to ask you to come to the dinner table a number of times, that would *not* be good listening.'

You might think your expectations are self-explanatory, but with kids it's never a safe assumption. Help your child meet your expectations by being specific and clear about what you want. If your littlie attends preschool, ask what language they use at preschool to address problem behaviours so you can use the same language at home. Using the same language across home and school will help you achieve change faster. And so everyone's on the same page, put behavioural goals in writing as well — pictures are better for littlies — and keep them somewhere visible. As well as making expectations clear, this should help keep behavioural goals front of mind.

For littlies, work on one behavioural goal at a time, and for older children, no more than two or possibly three goals, depending on the goals and your child's level of maturity. If your child has too many goals, they'll find it hard to achieve what you're asking of them, and too many goals will make it hard for you to be consistent in your response to misbehaviour as well. If there are multiple behaviours you want to address, prioritize, and once you've had success with your first goal, move on to the next goal. It might feel like a slower start, but working on too many goals at once will get you nowhere fast. When it comes to behaviour management, slow and steady wins the race.

One last important note. Make sure your expectations match your child's developmental level. Your child's behaviour might feel challenging, yet still be normal given their age. If you're frustrated because your five-year-old isn't able to get ready for school independently it's not challenging behaviour per se; it's a skills limitation normal for their age and level of development. Your child taking on more responsibility might be something *you're* ready for, but unless your expectations match what your *child's* ready for, things won't go to plan. To ensure success, make sure your expectations are realistic.

Give clear instructions

We're quick to blame kids for 'naughty' behaviour, but misbehaviour is often as much parent-driven as it is child-driven. Instructions are a perfect example. We might think we're communicating our expectations clearly, but the reality is often quite different. To us, comments like, 'I'm sick and tired of having to pick up after you all the time' might imply a request for cleanliness, but it's an indirect message and one that's easily missed by kids, especially younger kids who are still developing the communication skills they need to understand implied messages like this. An instruction that clearly states what's expected, like 'I'd like you to put your school shoes and school bag in your cupboard as soon as you walk in the door rather than leaving them lying in the hallway' is much clearer and leaves little room for misinterpretation. Clear communication also means giving a deadline. You might think your tone conveys that you want your request actioned now or in the not-too-distant future, but it's not a safe assumption. Setting a deadline is a safer bet. For younger kids, deadlines should be shorter to minimize the risk of forgetfulness, but older kids and tweens should be able to cope with a bit of leeway, for example, 'I need this done by lunchtime'.

Phrasing instructions as a question is another common error and one you might not be aware you're making. When instructions are phrased as questions, it weakens the strength of the instruction. Think of it this way: if your boss asked you whether you thought you needed to have a piece of work completed by a certain date, would that carry as much weight as if they told you that you had to have that piece of work completed by a certain date, period? Instructions phrased as questions — 'Do you think it's time for bed now?' — are confusing to kids. A straightforward, direct instruction — 'It's time for bed now. Go and put your pyjamas on please' — will always work better than a question-based instruction.

To be effective, your instructions also need to take your child's age into account. Requests like, 'Turn off the TV, brush your teeth, and finish packing your bag for school' might seem simple to you, but it's actually a pretty complex directive, especially if your child's younger. An instruction like this requires your child to manage the frustration they'll experience at having to stop something they're enjoying (you might not think turning the TV off is a big deal, but it is a big deal to your child): they have to be flexible enough to shift focus to a new activity; plan how to execute your request; keep the information they need to complete the task in their working memory; and stay focused long enough to get the job done.

After years of practice, your skills in these areas are highly developed. Not only that, your brain has matured and evolved to support these skills, so for you, a request like this is easy. Not so for your child. He or she is still learning and needs your help, and that means simplifying things and giving single-task instructions.

Lastly, if you're going to be effective, you need to gain your child's attention before you deliver an instruction. Yes, this means you have to stop what you're doing first. Is this inconvenient? Absolutely. The extra effort isn't ideal, but it'll help you be more effective, and the time you lose getting your child's attention will be well made up for in the time you save not having to repeat yourself 30 times. Try it and you'll see what I mean.

Give your child a chance to respond

The speed with which your child can take in, make sense of, and respond to information increases with age. Younger children in particular need more time to process information, though kids of all ages will be slower than you when it comes to responding to a request. It pays to be mindful of this when dishing out instructions. When you give an instruction, expect to repeat it at least once, but give your child at least five to ten seconds to respond before repeating your request. If your request relates to a safety-related behaviour — hitting, kicking, or biting for example — don't wait, act immediately, but for all other requests, give your child a chance to respond and at least one to two instruction repeats before you step in.

Past one or two repeats, don't continue to issue the same instruction over and over again. If your child hasn't taken action by the second reminder, odds are they're not going to, and continuing to repeat yourself only inadvertently teaches your child that they don't have to listen when you talk. Once you've reached your instruction threshold, stop what you're doing and monitor your child's completion of their task. Yes, it's a more time-consuming approach in the short-term, but nagging isn't a time-effective approach either. Invest in teaching your child that when you give an instruction you expect it to be actioned. It'll save you time in the long run.

Attend to positive behaviour, ignore misbehaviour

If your child's behaviour is attention driven, to change it you'll need to change which behaviours you're attending to. Remember, younger children in particular don't differentiate between positive and negative attention, so any attention — reprimands, yelling, chasing — can reinforce problem behaviour. Let's say your child is in the habit of throwing a tantrum when they can't have something they want. If each time this happens you patiently sit with your child to explain why they can't have what they want and why throwing a tantrum isn't acceptable, you might find nothing changes. Why? Because even though you're saying all the right things, the level of attention you're giving your child during and after their tantrum is drowning out your verbal messages.

Your attention is a powerful reinforcer, so for attention-driven behaviour the secret is this: give lots of attention and praise to the behaviour you want to see, and minimal or no attention to the behaviours you don't want to see. Stick to this consistently and you'll see results.

Quality time

I'm sure you already know that quality time with your child is important. You're probably also very busy and don't have much free time, but if your child's behaviour is testing your patience, quality time might be the solution. Think of it this way: imagine you have a friend in a long-term relationship with a partner who doesn't make time for her, but expects a lot in return. He likes things done a certain way at home and is particular about meals, household cleanliness, and the way his shirts are ironed. On top of that, he works long hours, is rarely home, and hardly ever does anything nice for your friend. Would you be encouraging your friend to do what her partner wants her to do, even though he doesn't make time for her or their relationship? Probably not.

Our willingness to comply with requests and favours in relationships is strongly influenced by the quality of our relationships, and kids are no different. Expecting your child to behave well and comply with your requests when you don't put effort into your relationship is unfair and unreasonable. And if you think your child should do what you say regardless simply because you're their parent, be honest — would you really go out of your way to follow the directives of someone who rarely gives you the time of day?

Regardless of age, spending quality time with your child will improve your relationship, and in turn, a stronger relationship will improve your child's behaviour. Life is busy and quality time is hard to find, but you don't have to dedicate copious amounts of time to quality time for it to have an impact. Small pockets of time where you give your child your undivided attention — yes, that means putting down your phone and turning off your other screens — and actively engaging with them is all your child really needs. If you're really pushed for time, normal daily activities can be turned into quality time. Instead of multitasking while you prepare dinner, ask your son or daughter to sit with you and catch you up on what's happening in their life. If they're interested in cooking with you, give them tasks to do while you chat and use this opportunity to praise them for helping. Alternatively, use time in the car to start a conversation about your child's life. Turn off the radio, ask open-ended questions about their day, and show an interest in what they tell you.

How you increase quality time with your child doesn't matter; it's the effort that's important. Telling your child how much you love them isn't enough if your actions don't support this. Make the time, it'll be worth it.

Offer choices

If a need for control underlies your child's misbehaviour, choices are a powerful tool. Yes, there are times when you can't and shouldn't offer choices — choices around bedtime, dinner, and school attendance, for example — but if your child is given the opportunity to feel like they have a say at other times, they'll be better able to tolerate these boundaries, and more likely to comply with requests in general as a result.

Choice is good, but too much choice can be an issue for younger children; it can cause kids to feel overwhelmed, which can also cause misbehaviour. So offer a maximum of two choices. For example, 'Would you like a tuna sandwich or a peanut butter sandwich for lunch?' or 'Would you like to wear your green T-shirt or your red T-shirt?' As kids get older, put more choices on the table and try to cast a wider net in terms of the areas you're willing to offer choice in. And as your child approaches their teenage years, try to let him or her make decisions independently without you putting options on the table first. Tweens, in particular, desperately want independence. Facilitating this where you can will help you achieve compliance in other areas.

An important caveat when it comes to offering choices: make sure you only put forward choices you're happy with. Offering a choice and reneging when your child picks the option you didn't want them to choose will only make things worse.

Teach replacement skills

To behave well, kids need to want to behave well. But they also need skills, like the ability to manage their emotions, skills in flexible thinking, and an ability to communicate needs verbally. If your child is missing skills in any of these areas, motivational strategies like rewards and consequences won't work, because a desire to behave well isn't the issue; lagging skills are.

If your child's misbehaviour occurs when they're frustrated or upset, odds are they need help developing emotion regulation skills (for more on how to help your child build skills in this area, see Chapter 2). If changes to plans or requests to stop one task and start another are recurring triggers, then skills for cognitive flexibility are probably needed (see skills for problem-solving, also in Chapter 2). And if your child uses misbehaviour to communicate, it's practising expressing needs with words that'll get the job done.

Littlies, in particular, often need help to learn to verbally express needs. When something happens they don't like, they default to tantrums to show they need help, but it's not an effective means of communication. For one thing, as parents we tend to get so distracted by tantrums that we forget to look at what's being communicated. As a result, we don't intervene to offer what's really needed: parent modelling and skills training.

Let's say your child's thrown a tantrum because another child has the toy he wants. Rousing on him for his tantrum might reinforce the distinction between appropriate and inappropriate behaviour, but it doesn't help him build the skills he needs to respond differently in the future. What will help build these skills is parent modelling of an alternate behavioural response, something like: 'I think you're frustrated because you want to play with the truck Sam's using. If you want a turn you need to say: "Can I have a turn next?" Then play with something else while you wait for your turn.'

Skills, whether for emotion regulation, flexible thinking, or communicating needs, are essential to positive behaviour. Make skills practice a priority in your parenting.

Introduce rewards

When it comes to changing behaviour, rewards are a powerful tool. Rewards aim to increase a child's motivation to behave well, so if there are other issues at play — lagging skills, for example — rewards in isolation won't work. That being said, they're a useful addition to most behaviour management plans. And before you object: no, if you start using rewards you won't be stuck with them forever. You'll need to phase out rewards once you've established a new pattern of behaviour, but you shouldn't have any issues doing this, especially if your transition to no rewards is a gradual one. Rewards are a means to an end, and they're an effective means. Don't be afraid to use them.

There are a few essential rules of thumb to follow for rewards to work. First, the rewards have to be meaningful and specific. Rewarding your child with fifteen minutes of extra reading time will have little to no impact if reading isn't something your child's interested in. An extra fifteen minutes of TV time, though, will be a different story. If you're unsure what will motivate your child, ask. They'll be more than happy to help you come up with a list of reward options. Just make sure you include small, medium and large reward options so you can match rewards to the size of the behavioural challenge. And keep in mind that rewards don't have to be money-based. Fifteen minutes of special time with Mum or Dad, a trip to the park, or getting to pick what's for dinner one night are good rewards too. When it comes to rewards, anything goes, so long as your child knows exactly what's an offer, and it's something your child wants, not something you want them to want.

To be effective, rewards also need to be immediate, especially if your child is five years or younger. At a practical level this isn't always possible — you might not able to drop everything to go to the park straight away, for example. But there are ways around this. IOU tokens are a great way to mitigate against a delayed reward. Ask your child to help you create tokens for each of the rewards you've agreed on, and when they achieve their behavioural goal, reward them immediately with a token they can 'cash in' later. But while an IOU token will buy you some time, sooner is still always better than later. Try to make good on your reward promises as soon as possible after your child meets their behavioural goal, and if you're using IOU tokens, that should still be no later than 72 hours after the fact.

Kids will find working towards the same reward over and over again boring, so it's also important to mix things up. For younger children, reward boxes work well. Keep a variety of reward items in a special box or tub and when your child achieves their goal, let them go 'rewards shopping' in the relevant box. You can have a separate box for small, medium and larger reward items. Rewards boxes work for older kids, too, keeping in mind you can have tokens as well as actual objects in each box.

Rewards also only work if you follow through. Promising a reward but only haphazardly making good on your end of the agreement will undercut the power of the strategy. Not only that, not following through also teaches your child that you don't mean what you say, which can have consequences for the effectiveness of other strategies. If you're not able to follow through with rewards, don't use them.

Track progress with a rewards chart

Unless you're working to a 1:1 behaviour-to-reward ratio (which on an ongoing basis is probably overkill) your child will need to meet their behaviour goal at least a few times over before they earn a reward. A rewards chart is a helpful way to track progress. You can purchase rewards charts online, charts don't need to be complicated, and kids often enjoy making their own. All you really need is a piece of paper with a table listing the days of the week so you can keep track of how many stickers/points your child has earned. Younger kids respond well to sticker and stamp-based charts — stickers or stamps are often reward enough for little ones — but older kids tend to not be as motivated by these, and will generally respond better to a point-based system. A point can be a tally on a score card or objects kept in a rewards chart jar, like individual pieces of Lego, Connect Four discs, ping pong balls or coloured straws. The idea being that your child needs to earn a certain number of stickers/stamps or points before they earn an extra reward.

Choosing the right reward schedule for a rewards chart is key to the effectiveness of this strategy. Give your child a stamp/sticker/point each and every time they achieve their behavioural goal, but have other rewards on offer as well: extra privilege time, special time with Mum or Dad, special activities, a toy, or purchasing music or an episode of a favourite TV show via Apple TV.

How many stamps/stickers/points your child needs to earn a specific reward will depend on the size of the reward. Smaller rewards should require fewer stamps/stickers/points, and larger rewards a higher number. But rewards charts generally work best with a mix of small, medium and large rewards on offer. Each time your child achieves their goal, give them a stamp/sticker/point, and they can decide along the way whether they want to cash them in for a smaller reward or save them up towards one of the bigger rewards.

The number of stamps/stickers/points for any given reward will also depend on your child's age and the degree of difficulty of the task. For younger children, a rewards chart will only work if a reward can be earned relatively quickly. As a general rule, younger kids should be able to earn a reward within the first two to three days of starting a rewards chart. Older kids will be able to tolerate a higher stamps/stickers/points rewards threshold, but they still shouldn't have to wait more than seven days for a reward, at least not initially. As kids start to make progress and the degree of task difficulty reduces, gradually increase the number of stamps/stickers/points needed to earn a reward. Continue to do this until rewards have been phased out; but even past this point, continue to reward positive behaviour with praise.

If the behavioural goal you've set relates to not doing something — for example, 'keep your hands and feet to yourself' — how frequently you reward positive behaviour (i.e. managing to *not* hit, kick or bite) will depend on how frequently the problem behaviour occurs. If your child demonstrates aggressive behaviour a few times each hour, for example, initially offer a sticker/stamp/point each hour. If the problem behaviour is less frequent, say once or twice per day, you can offer a sticker/stamp/point either twice daily — break the day into morning-to-lunchtime and lunchtime-to-bedtime — or just at the end of the day.

Reward chart apps

Younger children respond well to paper or cardboard reward charts. They like being able to see their progress, and when their rewards chart is displayed somewhere noteworthy, such as on the refrigerator or family notice board, it keeps behavioural goals front of mind. But paper and cardboard rewards charts aren't readily accessible when you're out and about, which is why some parents prefer reward chart apps. A few good examples are listed for you below.

- **iReward Chart** helps you keep track of good behaviour via an interactive rewards chart. You can select behavioural goals and rewards from built-in lists or customize goals and rewards to match your child's needs, including how many stars your child needs to earn per reward. Best of all, the app syncs across iOS devices and users can invite others to collaborate on a child's chart — a handy feature for separated or divorced parents who want to keep behaviour management consistent across both households.

- **KidzAward** is very easy to use. Kids can pick the token they'd like to receive to keep track of their behaviour, and behavioural goals and rewards can be customized on this app as well. Compared to medium and large reward items, fewer tokens are needed to earn small rewards, but the number of tokens needed for each reward category isn't fully customizable. To facilitate progress, the app sends daily push notifications to remind you to review progress with your child, which is a great feature if you're a busy parent.

- **Tally: A Goal Tracker** helps users keep track of how often they engage in certain behaviours. It was designed to help users create healthier habits, but can also be used as a tally for behavioural goals. The free version allows you to add three habits (which can be your behavioural goals) and then all you need to do is tap the counter each time your child is successful. The app will keep count for you, and the simple interface makes it appealing to kids as well. This app works well for older kids who might think sticker- and token-based apps are a bit babyish.

Use consequences

When they're used properly, consequences are another powerful strategy. Like rewards, consequences work best when they're meaningful, immediate and consistently followed through on. But it's also important for consequences to be planned, not reactive. Telling your child in the heat of the moment they've lost TV privileges for a month is likely to escalate rather than de-escalate challenging behaviour, especially if it's a consequence you've imposed without advanced warning. Not only that, but by setting a consequence for this length of time you also make life harder for yourself. Once you've set a consequence you need to enforce it every day for the full duration if you're going to preserve your parenting power. If you've set a month-long consequence, that's no easy task.

The most effective consequences are pre-planned and limited to a time period that matches both the behavioural breach and your child's level of development. For younger children, consequences of a shorter duration are sufficient — anywhere between five minutes and three hours. And periods of up to 24 to 48 hours usually work best for older children. Any longer than that and things start to come undone.

One important point to keep in mind when it comes to consequences: withdrawing privileges is far easier to enforce than extra chores. If you set unpacking the dishwasher as a consequence, for example, you inadvertently set yourself up for a power battle every time the dishwasher needs to be unpacked. Removing a gaming console, on the other hand, is much easier to enforce. More painful from a whinging point of view, but the set-and-forget nature of removing privileges makes follow-through on consequences like this a much simpler task.

If you do end up needing to enforce a chore-based consequence and find yourself stuck in a power battle — bring out a timer. Let your child know you're going to start timing and for each minute it takes them to start their task, they'll lose five minutes off a favourite activity, such as TV or electronics, but it can also be things like having to sit in the car and be ten minutes late to soccer training or a birthday party. Then ignore. Don't get drawn into a power struggle; just walk away. You can offer a prompt every now and then, something like: 'You've only lost ten minutes so far, there's still time to turn things around' or 'The sooner you choose to start, the less time you lose — you're in control.' But otherwise step back and let the consequence work for you.

As your child gets older, logical consequences will become your new best friend. Logical consequences work with littlies as well — if they throw a toy and it breaks, for example, not having that toy to play with anymore is a logical consequence. But as your child becomes more independent, the opportunity for him or her to learn through logical consequences increases as well. If dirty clothes don't get put in the clothes basket, they don't get washed. If homework isn't completed, they get in trouble at school. And if they forget to pass on a party invitation and something else gets scheduled at that time, they might not be able to go. Parent-directed consequences will continue to be a part of your parenting repertoire as your child develops, but logical consequences are more powerful and require less effort on your part. Make use of them where you can.

Try your hand at negotiation

Many parents struggle with the idea of negotiation because it runs counter to the usual 'You'll do as I say because I'm the parent' parenting philosophy. But if your child needs to feel in control to behave well, or if they're desperate for independence — which will happen more and more as your child enters the tween and teenage years — negotiation is one of the most powerful parenting strategies you have at your disposal, and one you should definitely use. There will be times when your child needs to go along with what you say without challenging you or your reasoning first, but if you make the effort to take their thoughts and feelings into consideration at other times, this'll be an easier task.

Consider the scenario below. Harley is just home from school and his dad wants him to do his homework.

66 Dad: Okay, it's time for homework, off you go.

Harley: But I just got home. Can't I have a break first?

Dad: No. Let's just get it done and out of the way. You can have a break once you've finished.

Harley: *(frustrated Dad's not listening, starts to enter a stubborn mindset)* I don't want to do it now. I don't have that much to do anyway. I can just do it later.

Dad: *(feeling annoyed that Harley won't do as he's asked)* Well if you don't have much to do it won't take you long to do it now, will it?

Harley: *Stares defiantly at Dad with no intention of getting his school books out.*

Should Harley do as he's been asked to do? Of course he should. Is he going to? No. And persisting with a 'You'll do your homework because I've said you will' approach isn't going to help Harley's dad achieve the outcome he wants.

In this instance, negotiation is a better strategy.

66 Dad: Okay, it's time for homework, off you go.

Harley: But I just got home. Can't I have a break first?

66 Dad: *(would prefer Harley do his homework now, but knows forcing the issue won't be an effective approach)* I can understand you want a bit of a break after being at school all day. I'm just worried that once you start playing video games you won't want to stop and we'll end up fighting about homework, which I hate.

Harley: *(feeling listened to and understood, and more willing to listen in return as a result)* I don't have much homework today. Can I just do it later?

Dad: *(not completely opposed to Harley having a break first, but feeling the need for a firmer plan than 'later')* I can understand you want a break, but I think we need a set plan to follow so we don't end up fighting. It's 4 p.m. now, if you have a break, what time will you start your homework?

Harley: 4.30 p.m.

Dad: Okay, that could work. And how will we keep track of time so you know when to start?

Harley: I can set the timer on the microwave.

Dad: Okay, good idea. I still think we might end up fighting about stopping your game when it's time, though. How about you have a break and watch TV and when the show changes at 4:30 p.m., that's when I'll turn it off. Then when you've finished your homework, you can play your video game.

Harley: *(would prefer to play video games over TV, but also really wants a break; takes time to mull this over)* Okay.

Dad: Okay, great. I'll start the timer.

Negotiating with your child will feel backwards at first, but it's a powerful strategy and one that works particularly well with older kids. It won't undercut your parenting power; it'll strengthen it. Don't dismiss it before you try it.

A note on time out

You might notice I haven't included time out as one of the strategies I'd recommend for improving behaviour, and there's a reason. Time out can be a really effective strategy, but it can also be hit and miss. If your child readily complies with your requests to go to time out, there's nothing wrong with having a designated time out area — so long as the amount of time your child has to stay in time out matches their developmental level. However, if you have to chase your child around the house to get them to time out, or if you have to constantly return them to time out because they've given themselves an early mark, you may end up inadvertently reinforcing challenging behaviour, and this will make things worse.

If it works for you, keep using it, but if implementing time out creates more problems than it solves, try using age-appropriate consequences instead.

And one more on keeping rewards and consequences separate

Rewards and consequences are both good strategies and work best when they're used together, but it's essential to keep them separate. Rewarding your child with the chance to earn back a withdrawn privilege might seem like a good idea, especially if it helps to reduce whinging, but it'll work against you longer term. Ultimately, your child will learn that consequences are fairly innocuous because they can be reversed relatively easily, and this will undercut the power of any future consequences.

When it comes to parenting strategies, there's not an unlimited supply. Don't invalidate the few at your disposal by using them incorrectly.

Putting it into practice

When it comes to developing a behaviour management plan, which strategies you use will depend on the underlying cause of your child's misbehaviour and your child's age, but rewards should nearly always be part of your plan, especially if consequences are in play. Getting the right fit is also essential. If you use the wrong strategy or fail to adapt the strategy correctly for your child's age, your intervention won't be effective, and could make things worse — definitely not a desirable outcome.

Once you have your plan, which might include a combination of strategies, implement it consistently for two to three weeks before you decide whether it's working. Simpler behavioural issues should start to improve within that time, but if lagging skills are part of the problem, expect things to take a little longer. Learning new skills is a process, and your child will need time to practise their new skills before this practice translates into behavioural change.

And because consistency is key to any behaviour management program, if you're not able to be consistent (which is sometimes the case; life with kids can get pretty hectic) that's okay, but adjust your expectations on timeframes for progress. You'll still make progress, it'll just be slower. Be as consistent as you can, and be patient.

A couple of helpful pointers

Consistency between parents is just as important as individual consistency, so get the other half of your parenting team on board. If other people are involved in your child's care — step-parents, grandparents, a nanny — they'll need to be brought into the loop as well.

Know that people will only follow through with what you're asking of them if 1) they have a clear understanding of *why* you're implementing a behaviour management plan, and 2) they agree with your approach. So check in with the key players in your parenting team to gauge their level of agreement and any concerns. You might know what's best for your child, but if you skip this step, your efforts might be undone by a rogue parent or parenting team member. It's not uncommon, for example, for one parent to be overly permissive and easy going in reaction to feeling that their other parenting half is being overly strict, and vice versa. If there are differences in opinion, find a middle ground. Your chances of success are far greater if everyone is on the same page.

When you're implementing a behaviour management plan it's also important to prime your child for success. If you know you're entering a situation that usually triggers challenging behaviour, plan ahead and remind your child of their goals and the rewards and consequences at play beforehand. At the start of each day, prompt your child to remember what they're working towards and exactly what they have to do to earn their rewards. And when your child has a lapse, help them get back on track as quickly as possible. The more time you invest in helping your child to behave well, the greater your chance of success.

When you're not seeing progress

If nothing improves, one of two things is happening: you think you're executing strategies correctly, but you're not, in which case you need to double-check what you're doing and how consistently you're doing it; or you're addressing some, but not all of the underlying causes, which means there are factors at play that haven't yet been addressed, and you need to take another look at what that could be.

Take Brittany and Mark. Their son Jacob is ten, and he's putting his parents through the wringer at bedtime.

> " Every night it's the same thing. After trying every excuse in the book, from forgotten homework to dire thirst, when we finally get him to bed he doesn't want us to leave the room. After an hour of negotiating extra reading time, when we do finally manage to leave, he'll stay in bed for fifteen minutes before coming down and telling us he can't sleep. Some nights it takes three to four hours to get him to bed.
>
> We've tried everything. Jacob really wanted a new computer game, but it's quite expensive so in the past we've said no, but out of

desperation I told him that if he went to bed without any fuss for a month, I'd buy it for him. It seemed to work for a few nights, but then things went backwards again. We've tried sitting with him until he falls asleep, letting him stay up a bit later in case it made him tireder at bedtime, and talking to him about why he can't go to sleep on his own, but he doesn't really seem to know.

Jacob used to be a really good sleeper. He slept through the night from six months and hasn't given us any trouble since. He had a nasty stomach bug recently, so we let him sleep in our room for a while, but that was months ago. He's not sick — we've taken him to the paediatrician and had everything checked out. So I really don't understand why he won't sleep. We've tried to be patient, we really have, but we both have really demanding jobs and work really long hours.

What's frustrating for Brittany and Mark is that despite the huge amount of effort they're putting in, they're not having any real success. They have the right intention, they're trying to implement strategies to improve Jacob's behaviour at bedtime, but the strategies don't match the underlying cause of Jacob's behaviour, and even though they've got the right idea with using rewards, they've made a few errors in execution, which are undermining the effectiveness of this strategy.

Jacob's not a 'naughty' kid and his current behaviour is out of character, so there's a reason why he's misbehaving. Brittany and Mark started to explore possible causes for Jacob's behaviour. They took him to their paediatrician and ruled out physical causes, but their search stopped there. Had they looked further and thought more about when Jacob's bedtime antics started — which to be fair, they might have thought to do if they weren't so tired — they might have noticed that things started to go south after Jacob was allowed to sleep in his parents' room while he was unwell. Jacob isn't being difficult because he's suddenly turned into a delinquent; his behaviour has changed because he's seeking from his parents what he had while he was sick — empathy, care and attention.

Like many parents, Jacob's parents work long hours. They're tired when they get home and find it hard to stop thinking about work deadlines and outstanding tasks. They try not to be, but they're often on their phones outside work hours, checking emails. Because they're in work mode in the evenings, they're not always present in their interactions with Jacob. When Jacob was sick, though, that all changed. Both parents stopped everything to look after Jacob, and he was given lots of love and attention. It'd be a stretch to say he enjoyed being sick, but for Jacob, being sick definitely had its advantages.

What Jacob wants is time with his parents. And that's why Brittany and Mark's current approach isn't working. By letting Jacob stay up past his bedtime and sitting with him until he falls asleep, without meaning to, they're teaching Jacob to misbehave at bedtime, because they're reinforcing his bedtime refusal with the time and attention he craves. If Brittany and Mark want things to change, they're going to need to find time to have quality time with Jacob earlier in the evening so he doesn't turn to challenging behaviour at bedtime to get this need met.

If Jacob still plays up at bedtime initially, even though he's getting special time with Brittany and Mark earlier in the day, Brittany and Mark should return Jacob to bed with minimal conversation, just 'It's time for bed now', each and every time he leaves his room, and this should help things settle down. They may need to be prepared to return Jacob to his room ten or even twenty times in the first few nights while he tests these new boundaries, but if they stick to their plan, Jacob should go back to being a good sleeper in no time.

In terms of rewards, Brittany and Mark had the right idea trialling this strategy, but a few slight errors in their execution undermined its effectiveness. For example, the behavioural goal they'd set — 'Go to bed without a fuss' — isn't clear and leaves room for misinterpretation. A more specific goal, like 'Go to bed when Mum and Dad ask, accept when Mum and Dad need to leave the room after fifteen minutes of reading, and stay in bed until it's time to get up the next day', is more clear-cut and would help Jacob to have a clearer idea of what's expected. And while the reward Jacob's working towards is obviously one he really wants, which is perfect, for a ten-year-old, a month is a long time to have to wait for a reward and probably why Jacob lost motivation after just a few nights. Using a rewards chart to track progress and small- and medium-sized rewards to bridge the gap between now and Jacob's bigger end-of-month reward would likely help to sustain Jacob's interest and motivation, increasing the likelihood of success.

Max is four years old and his parents, Sue and Michael, are at their wits' end. Max attends preschool five days per week and last week Sue and Michael were asked to attend a meeting with the preschool director after Max behaved aggressively towards another child.

" It was such an awkward meeting. Max bit another child and the other parents complained. Of course they did, it's appalling behaviour and I can't believe he did it. I wish I could say it's an isolated event but it's not. I dread pick-up because I know I'm going to get ambushed and pulled in for 'a quick chat'. He belted a kid earlier this week because he wouldn't share a toy they both wanted, and yesterday he pulled a little girl's hair because she wouldn't let him use her crayons. I'm so embarrassed and worried he's going to start getting known as the 'naughty kid', and I really don't want that for him. It might not be related, but one of the kids in his class had a birthday party last weekend and everyone else in the class was asked, but not Max. I'm worried it's because people are too afraid to have him around their kids, which is so frustrating, because he's actually a really sweet little boy. He's really loving and caring. I don't know what's going on.

He doesn't ever act this way at home so we've probably been a bit slow to do anything about it. His preschool has tried a rewards chart, but it doesn't seem to have helped. They told Max they wanted to help him learn how to keep his hands and feet to himself and explained that he'd get a sticker if he was able to do so for the day. At the start of each day they'd remind Max about his goal — I think they gave him reminders through the day as well — and if he could stick to his goal, he'd earn a special award and sticker for the day that he could show me at pick-up. And he'd also get to pick a reward from the rewards box at home. It was a really good plan, but he's only earned one sticker in the last two weeks. I thought at first that maybe we weren't offering good enough rewards, but he's always really upset when he doesn't get a sticker and can't pick a reward from the rewards box. His teachers act quickly when he's aggressive — he gets asked to sit out of playtime — so I don't know why he's acting this way. We're worried that if we don't get to the bottom of this soon, his preschool will ask us to leave.

Max plays really well with his brother, Lucas, who's six, which makes what's happening at preschool so confusing. Lucas is a pretty easy-going kid and is great with Max. If Max wants to play a certain game, Lucas goes along with it, and if Max wants a turn of what Lucas is doing, he's happy to give him a go.

The rewards chart plan Sue and Michael developed with Max's preschool was a good one and he seems motivated by the rewards on offer, so all in all there don't seem to be too many issues with the way the reward chart is being used. Given that Max is showing signs of aggression on a daily basis, progress might be helped by giving him stickers more frequently — by breaking the day into morning to mid-morning, mid-morning to mid-afternoon, mid-afternoon to end of day for example — but there's another reason Max's parents aren't seeing much progress.

Sue and Michael have forgotten to look at the why. They've jumped straight to assuming Max is choosing to be naughty without looking at what other factors might be at play. Max is misbehaving for a reason. He's having trouble managing frustration and expressing his needs appropriately, which is why his poor behaviour has continued despite meaningful rewards.

What Max needs is emotion skills training (see Chapter 2 for more information on this) and someone to prompt appropriate behaviour. Asking Max to sit out of playtime is helpful in that it sends an immediate message that his behaviour isn't acceptable, but it doesn't help him to know what he should do instead — and that's the missing piece of the puzzle. Max needs someone to intervene and help him to practise expressing his needs verbally so he doesn't have to rely on his behaviour to communicate his frustration. What that would look like is something like this:

> 66 Teacher/parent: Max, I think you hit Alex because you wanted to play with the train set he was using. It's not okay to hit. If you'd like a turn you need to say, 'Can I have a turn please?' then play with another toy until it's your turn.

Even though Max isn't behaving poorly at home, there's a reason: his patience isn't ever tested. If Max wants something, his older brother gives it to him, and Sue and Michael don't intervene to make Max wait his turn. This helps to keep the peace in the short term, but what Sue and Michael don't realize is that they're inadvertently stopping Max from having the experiences he needs to learn how to tolerate frustration and use words to express his needs. Lucas might be happy to cave in to Max's demands, but Max's peers at preschool are playing by a different set of rules. This pattern of interaction at home also needs to change if Max is going to learn the skills he needs to behave well. It'll mean more tantrums at home in the short term, but it'll also mean improved behaviour and better peer relationships longer term.

When you're doing everything right and things still don't improve

If you've covered all your bases in terms of possible underlying causes of misbehaviour and you've been diligent in your applications of strategies and know you're using them correctly and you're still not seeing any progress, it might be time to look at other less common causes, like Attention Deficit Hyperactivity Disorder (ADHD) and Oppositional Defiant Disorder (ODD).

There's been a lot written about ADHD, some of it accurate, some of it wildly inaccurate. ADHD is a neurodevelopmental disorder characterized by deficits in three key areas: attention, hyperactivity and impulsivity. Kids with untreated ADHD are easily distracted and have difficulty staying on task. They find it hard to plan ahead and start tasks when they're supposed to, and they can act impulsively without any thought for consequences, not because they're naughty, but because their prefrontal cortex — the control centre of the brain, and the part responsible for managing executive function skills — is under-active and not functioning in the way it should.

Dr Thomas Brown, author of *Attention Deficit Disorder: The unfocused mind in children and adults*, compares the prefrontal cortex to the conductor of an orchestra, and the various executive function skills — the ability to resist distractions and stay focused on a task, for example — to the musicians. As he says, it's not that children with ADHD don't have executive function skills; they do, they just have trouble executing these skills at the right times. They're missing a conductor, someone to organize things so the right skills are activated and brought into use in the right way at the right time.

Even parents with excellent parenting skills find parenting a child with ADHD challenging. ADHD is a neurological condition, the result of deficits in brain function, which is why medication is often an essential part of any treatment protocol. Medications for ADHD act to stimulate the brain to boost functioning in those parts — the prefrontal cortex — that are underactive. It can be scary to give your child medication, especially when they're young, but not giving your child medication when they need it could cause additional problems — friendship issues, academic problems and issues with low self-esteem are all common in kids with untreated ADHD.

If your child had diabetes, you wouldn't expect them to will themselves to produce more insulin. You'd give them the insulin injections they need. Expecting a child with ADHD to will themselves to correct their brain function isn't fair either. Whether or not you end up giving your child medication is a decision only you can make, and you know your child best, but if medication is recommended to you by a health professional, be open to considering a trial and make sure any decisions you make about medication are based on facts, not misinformation and hype.

How is ADHD diagnosed?

While ADHD isn't a diagnosis to be jumped to at the first sign of challenging behaviour, it's a very real condition and one that should be explored if you're having significant behavioural difficulties. According to the *Diagnostic and Statistical Manual of Mental Disorders* (DSM-5), to be diagnosed with ADHD, a child must have experienced symptoms of inattention and/or hyperactivity-impulsivity for at least six months. For a formal diagnosis, symptoms must also: have been present before twelve years of age, be occurring in more than just one setting, and be interfering with social and academic functioning or development.

Symptoms considered for diagnoses include:
- doesn't pay close attention to details or makes careless mistakes in schoolwork or other activities
- often finds it hard to maintain attention
- your child often might not seem to listen when spoken to directly
- often does not follow through on instructions and fails to finish schoolwork or other tasks
- they will often find it difficult to organize activities or tasks
- your child will often avoid or be reluctant to take part in tasks requiring sustained mental effort (like homework)
- often loses things
- is easily distracted (including by unrelated thoughts)
- is often forgetful about everyday things like chores or notes from school.

Hyperactive-impulsive symptoms include if your child often:
- fidgets with or taps hands or feet or squirms in their seat
- leaves their seat when remaining seated is expected
- runs about or climbs at inappropriate times

- can't play quietly
- is 'on the go'
- talks excessively
- gives an answer before the question is finished
- has difficulty waiting his or her turn
- interrupts, butts into conversations, starts using other people's things without asking or receiving permission.

If you think your child might have ADHD, speak to your general practitioner and ask for a referral to a paediatrician or a child and adolescent clinical psychologist. Be prepared, though: unless your child's behaviour is at the severe end of the spectrum, few health professionals will be willing to consider an ADHD diagnosis in children younger than seven — and for good reason. Executive function skills are still developing in young children and slow development of these skills could be what's driving the misbehaviour. An ADHD diagnosis is also just that: a diagnosis, not a solution. If your child is diagnosed with ADHD, their behaviour will be easier to understand, but still frustrating to deal with. Engage with a good clinical psychologist and paediatrician and get the right support.

When nothing you're doing seems to be working, Oppositional Defiant Disorder or ODD is another diagnosis to consider. ODD is a behavioural disorder usually first diagnosed in childhood. It can be diagnosed at any age, but ODD-type behaviours are usually noticeable from about eight years of age.

ODD is characterized by a persistent pattern of disruptive behaviour — including being deliberately annoying, uncooperative, vindictive, argumentative, disobedient and defiant. While no one knows exactly what causes ODD, temperament (especially a temperament that makes a child more emotionally reactive and less able to tolerate frustration) and parenting issues (inconsistent discipline or a lack of parental supervision, for example) are likely risk factors.

Living with a child who's rude, disrespectful and oppositional in almost every situation is exhausting, and constant defiance will make it easy to fall into the trap of thinking your child's solely to blame. But generally speaking, family dynamics also play a role, even if just in maintaining symptoms. Relentless oppositional behaviour understandably triggers heated arguments and negativity from other family members, and while reactions like this are completely understandable, they also often make symptoms worse, which is why family-based and parenting interventions are the most effective treatment. With the right treatment, kids with ODD can make positive progress, but when ODD is left untreated, things usually get worse, and symptoms often continue into adulthood.

How do I know if my child has ODD?

All kids can be painful at times but the behaviour of kids with ODD is consistently challenging. To differentiate between normal challenging behaviour and ODD-related behaviour, the DSM-5 stipulates that to meet criteria for a diagnosis, the frequency and intensity of the challenging behaviour must be more than what is considered normal for a child's developmental level. As a guide, it's suggested that kids younger than five must show symptoms most days for a period of at least six months, and kids five years or older should demonstrate challenging behaviour at least weekly for six months or more. If you're concerned, a good paediatrician or clinical psychologist are your best first point of contact.

DSM-5 criteria for ODD

A pattern of behaviour lasting at least six months, that includes at least four symptoms listed below, displayed when interacting with at least one person who isn't a sibling.

- **Angry or irritable mood:** often loses temper; is easily annoyed or touchy; is often resentful or angry.
- **Argumentative or defiant:** argues with adults; actively defies the rules; deliberately annoys people; blames others for their mistakes or behaviour.
- **Vindictiveness:** has been vindictive or spiteful at least twice in the last six months.

The important bits

+ Rest assured, *all* kids go through periods of challenging behaviour, even kids with excellent parents.

+ It's easy to blame kids for misbehaviour, but to be effective, be open to the possibility that you might be part of the problem as well.

+ To be effective in improving your child's behaviour, you need to have a clear understanding of why they're misbehaving.

+ It pays to remember that your child's brain is still developing and the skills he or she needs to behave well are still developing, too.

+ Behaviour management strategies will only be effective if: a) they address the underlying cause of your child's misbehaviour, b) they're executed correctly, and c) they've been adapted correctly to meet your child's age and developmental level.

+ When it comes to implementing strategies, consistency is key. Make sure all adults involved in your child's care are across and willing to stick to your behaviour management plan.

+ If you're doing everything correctly and nothing's working, consider exploring other possible explanations like ADHD or ODD with your paediatrician or a child and adolescent clinical psychologist.

2

WHEN YOUR CHILD'S MELTDOWNS ARE DRIVING YOU UP THE WALL

The raging tantrums that are synonymous with the terrible twos are generally accepted as a passing phase, and tolerated on the understanding that, at this age, your little one can't express their needs in any other way. Fast forward a few years, though, and things are a little different. Your child's tantrums have grown to be more dramatic and explosive, and your empathy's starting to wane. You were able to understand and make allowances for your eighteen-month-old's meltdowns without too much difficulty, but your ten-year-old's? Not so much. Their outbursts seem wholly disproportionate to both their age and the situation at hand — uncontrollable sobbing over a cancelled play date, explosive anger in reaction to homework prompts, and complete devastation at the thought of screen time being cut short. But as much as it feels like your child's tantrums are a deliberate attempt to bring you undone, there's a little more to it than that.

Just like when they were younger, your child's current meltdowns are a sign they need your help. Unlike when they were younger, your child's now old enough to learn skills to self-regulate. They're going to need your help, and a whole truckload of your patience, but there's a lot you can do to help your child develop the skills they need to keep their emotions in check. To be an effective teacher, you're going to need to let go of your frustration and be in the right mindset, though, and it starts with having a better understanding of what's happening.

Recent research suggests that differences in emotional reactivity between kids and adults might be due to changes in the relationship between the amygdala (the part of the brain responsible for emotion processing and emotional expression) and the prefrontal cortex (the more logical, reason-based part of the brain) across development.

At the forefront of research in this area is Nim Tottenham, Professor of Psychology at Columbia University, Associate Professor at the Child Study Center at Yale School of Medicine, and Director of the Developmental Affective Neuroscience Laboratory. Professor Tottenham and her team are interested in the development of the amygdala and its related neural circuitry, and in particular how this neural circuitry might support the learning of emotion regulation skills. In a recent study, Professor Tottenham and her team had participants (children, adolescents, and young adults aged between four and 22) undergo functional brain scans to measure activity in the amygdala and prefrontal cortex while they viewed pictures of people with happy, neutral or fearful facial expressions, the latter of which in particular is known to trigger an amygdala response.[1]

While all participants showed an amygdala response to fearful faces, amygdala reactivity was far stronger in children — especially children under ten — than in teens or young adults, and this decrease in amygdala reactivity across age corresponded with a change in the functional relationship between the amygdala and the prefrontal cortex. In teens and young adults, the prefrontal cortex functioned to regulate the activity of the amygdala, potentially accounting for the lower levels of amygdala reactivity in these age groups. In children under ten, though, this functional relationship didn't exist.

What this research seems to suggest is that a child's brain is vastly different from an adult's brain. Whereas adult brains are wired with strong functional connections between the amygdala and prefrontal cortex, children's brains aren't. The connections between the emotional and rational parts of their brains are only just starting to develop, and it's this shortfall in connectivity that increases their vulnerability for emotional mishaps.

The take-home is this: your child's meltdowns might be excessive and unreasonable, but they're not deliberate. The neural scaffolding your child needs to manage big emotions is still developing, and this makes it hard for them to keep big emotions in check. The good news is, your child will get better at regulating their emotions naturally as they develop the neural connectivity they need to support this skill, but the maturation process is a long one, so brain plasticity is your saving grace. Our brains, and your child's brain in particular, are incredibly plastic, meaning they're clever enough to adapt and change in response to new experiences. When your child practises new skills — like the skills they need for emotion regulation — the neural connections needed to support these skills are established and strengthened, and these new neural connections help to support skill mastery.

You don't have to wait for development to run its course. Through skills practice, your child can learn to better manage their emotions now, but they need your help. Their skills practice needs to be driven by you, at least initially. The more you help your child practise, the faster they'll learn. This means more work for you up front, but think about how much time you waste already on tantrums and the post-tantrum fallout. You're already doing the hard yards, but your efforts aren't translating into behavioural change. Invest in teaching your child the skills they need to cope with their emotions. The household peace alone will make it worth it.

Skills training pre-requisites

To successfully manage emotion-based meltdowns, you need to be able to time your intervention right, be a wizard at emotional validation, and know how to balance validation with boundary-setting. Fail to nail these three things and it won't matter how proactive you are in encouraging your child's skills practice, you won't see results.

Read each section below carefully, covering the pre-requisite skills, and make sure you're clear on how to put each into action before moving on.

Catch feelings early

Once your child's in full meltdown mode, logic gives way to emotion, and skills practice becomes near impossible, so you'll need to help them catch their feelings early. An emotion-based traffic light system is usually pretty effective and works for most ages, but whether it'll work for your three- or four-year-old will depend on your child. Try explaining to your littlie how a traffic light system works, and if they grasp the concept, great, but if they don't, introduce them to the idea of different levels of intensity in emotion by talking about big and small feelings — for example, 'I think when I took your truck away it gave you a big angry feeling' — and come back to a traffic light system when they're a bit older.

For kids who are ready, introduce an emotion-based traffic light system by saying something like the following.

> **"** I've noticed you've been having a hard time managing your frustration lately. You're not in trouble and I'm not mad, everyone has trouble managing big feelings sometimes, but I know you don't feel good when your feelings take over, so I want to help you learn how to boss your feelings back.
>
> See this picture of a set of traffic lights? I know you know that in traffic, a green light means you're good to go, a yellow light means you need to start to slow down, and a red light means you need to stop until the light turns green again. We're going to use traffic lights like this to learn how to be the boss of your feelings. Green means everything's all good, you're relaxed, happy and in control; yellow means you're starting to feel a bit frustrated or upset but you're still mostly in control; and red means you're feeling really

angry or upset and your feelings are starting to take over, making you say and do things that might get you in trouble.

Once your child understands how an emotion-based traffic light system works, work together to figure out how he or she will know if they're green, yellow or red. If your child has a pretty good understanding of their emotions, this will be an easy task, but younger kids or kids who are still developing their emotion skills may need a bit of extra help figuring out their yellow and red warning signs. If that's the case, spend a week or so (longer if needed) doing a bit of research. When you see that your child's starting to get frustrated or upset, ask them to identify what they're thinking and feeling, what physical sensations they can feel in their body, and record what they do when they're frustrated and upset. Keep at it until your child has at least two to three signs for when they're yellow and red.

Learning to catch feelings early is a tricky skill, but it's one of the most important skills to master for emotion regulation. If your child isn't aware they're yellow until it's too late, the likelihood of them being able to implement skills and strategies to calm down is slim to none. Your child will need help to catch their feelings early, so don't task them with the impossible goal of self-reflecting independently or you'll be setting them up to fail. Keep a close eye on your child and when you notice their yellow signs, intervene.

Validate, validate, validate

When your child's hysterical over something as trivial as it being time to head home from the park, it can be hard to take their distress seriously. Finding any kind of empathy is harder again when you're dealing with your own adult stressors, and stressors that have actual, real-life consequences at that. Comparatively speaking, limits on TV time, bath time, and being 'forced' to eat less-preferred foods aren't really in the same ballpark as demanding work deadlines, mortgage stress and family problems. But dismissing your child's feelings on the basis that the situations causing their distress are less stressful than the ones you're facing isn't really fair, and it's definitely not going to help you to be effective. If anything, it'll make things worse. The distress your child feels when they face their stressors is the same level of distress you feel when you face yours, only you have skills to cope with your distress — your child is still learning.

Respecting your child's feelings, no matter what caused them, will go a long way towards your child feeling heard and understood. It's as much about being effective as anything else. Think about what you respond to best when you're upset. Would you respond well if the friend you were venting to started lecturing you about the ridiculousness of your reaction, or would you just feel plain pissed off? I'd put my money on the latter. There's no way you'd respond well to that, and rightly so. Your child isn't any different.

When you tell your child they're being ridiculous when they're upset, two things happen. You instantly escalate your child's distress, because now they're also upset because you don't understand them; and you as good as guarantee your child's going to stay distressed for a while — at least in the short-term — just so they can prove how legitimate and valid their distress really is. On the other hand, when you validate how your child feels, you circumvent this. Your child feels heard and understood, so you side-step any potential escalations. And because you've managed to keep their distress contained, with a bit of extra help, they can let go of their frustration and shift more easily from a problem-focused to a solution-focused mindset.

Validating your child's distress is a powerful strategy that might feel backwards, especially if they're behaving poorly, but be open to giving it a try. It'll mean letting go of adult biases and trying to see things from your child's point of view, which might take some practice, but the results will be worth it.

Balance validation with limit setting

When your child's losing their mind because you've said no to a request, it's easy to fall into the trap of assuming their tantrum is a tactical one to try to convince you to change your mind. That might be a small part of the equation, but odds are your child's also genuinely distressed over not being able to have something they desperately want.

When your child's genuinely distressed, understanding, emotional validation and parent-driven emotion regulation skills practice need to be part of your response. Turning a blind eye or leading with consequences won't work, because attention and indifference aren't the issue; lagging skills are. That's not to say limits aren't important, but when it comes to distress-based tantrums, a two-pronged approach is key.

Let's say your child's mad — and has made that clear by wreaking havoc in the living room — because the afternoon play date he was looking forward to has been cancelled by the other family. You're mad as well because you'd spent the morning organizing the now dishevelled living room.

> **"** You: What are you doing!?! Stop it right now. I can't believe you've made such a mess.
>
> Child: I want to go to Sam's house.
>
> You: Well you can't, I've already told you that, and that's no reason to throw things around like this! Clean this mess up, right now.
>
> Child: *(storms off feeling misunderstood, confused by big feelings, and frustrated)*
>
> Parent: Get back here! If you don't clean this mess up right now you can forget having any more play dates.

No one wins in this scenario. You're upset and frustrated, your child's upset and frustrated, and the living room is still a mess. Your child needs help understanding his emotions. He's been looking forward to his play date and he's really disappointed it's not happening. He doesn't have the skills to tell you this, so he's wrecked the living room instead. Do you give him a hug and ignore the tantrum that made everything such a mess? No, of course not, that'll only teach him that poor behaviour when he's upset is acceptable, which it's not. But if you want him to learn to manage his emotions differently, you also need to not make sure poor behaviour isn't your only focus.

Your child needs you to take his feelings seriously and show him you understand. He also needs you to tell him that his feelings make sense and are completely understandable in light of what's occurred. Showing him you understand will go a long way towards helping him to let go of his disappointment, and as a result he'll be more able to acknowledge that his response wasn't so great. He'll also be more open to practising what he could have done instead, and skills practice like this is ultimately how he'll learn to do things differently next time.

> **You:** What are you doing!?! Stop it right now. I can't believe you've made such a mess.
>
> **Child:** I want to go to Sam's house.
>
> **You:** *(still furious, but aware child's behaviour is distress-based, so resist the urge to react angrily, and take a deep breath instead)* I know you've been looking forward to seeing Sam all week and you're really disappointed they've called to cancel. It's really disappointing and hard when plans change like that. I can understand why you're frustrated.
>
> **Child:** *(calmer because he feels heard and understood, stops what he's doing to listen)*
>
> **You:** *(working overtime to be patient, calm, and understanding)* I'm sorry you can't see Sam today like you wanted to; is there anything we could do that would help you to feel better? I know you've been wanting to go to the park to practise your scootering — we could do that instead? Or is there anything else you'd like to do today?
>
> **Child:** *(brightening up)* Can we go to the park?

You: *(still annoyed, but relieved to have avoided a tantrum)* You bet. And we can call Sam's mum to see if we can organize another play date for next weekend.

Child: *(still slightly disappointed, but much happier and calmer than before)*

You: *(knowing destructive behaviour still needs to be addressed)* There's something we need to do first though ...

Child: *(looking sheepish)* Tidy my mess?

You: Yep. I know you felt frustrated and upset and you had every right to feel that way, but it's not okay to throw things. Put things back where they belong and then we can go to the park.

Child: Okay.

Of course, if a tantrum involves physical aggression or any other safety-based behaviour — running away, for example — you'll need to reverse your approach. Respond with consequences immediately, then later, once things have calmed down, come back to validate any underlying emotions and look at what your child could do differently next time. But if safety isn't an issue, validate first and make consequences a secondary focus.

Teach skills for managing emotions — effectively

If your child's meltdowns are distress-based, behaviour-based strategies like rewards charts or deliberate ignoring in isolation aren't going to work, because your child's meltdowns aren't due to a lack of motivation to behave well or a need for attention: they're the result of still developing emotion regulation skills.

To stop having meltdowns, your child needs help learning skills to manage big emotions, and these skills — and how to teach them — are outlined below. Your child might need help to learn all of them, or they might have mastered a few but need help with others. Gauge your child's level of expertise in each, then use the information below to fill in their skills gaps.

How you execute emotion-focused strategies (and how you time your intervention) will either help or hinder your success, so before you do anything develop a plan of attack. Look at which skills your child needs help learning, know your child's yellow and red warning signs, and make sure you have a good understanding of which strategies to use and when before you start. Rushing over this part might help you feel more on top of things initially, but it'll slow your progress in the long run. Take the time to develop a clear plan from the outset and use it to keep you on task and consistent.

A green skill: help your child identify their emotions

As an adult, you've had lots of time to get to know your emotions, but your child hasn't had nearly as much practice, so for them, identifying feelings — and big feelings in particular — is a more challenging task.

Being able to identify and talk about feelings is an important skill your child needs to master before they can learn other emotion regulation skills. If your child's a bit older, they can probably label their emotions quite easily, but younger kids are still getting to know their feelings, and may need extra help. You can help them learn about their feelings by labelling emotions for them, for example, 'I think you're feeling frustrated because you can't find where that piece of the puzzle goes' and by labelling feelings of characters in books: 'Look, I think that boy is sad because he can't play with the ball.' For younger kids, extend things further by talking about the physical and behavioural symptoms of emotions, for example, 'I think you're frustrated because you can't work out where that piece of the puzzle goes. I can tell you're frustrated because your arms are crossed, your face looks angry and you don't normally slam puzzle pieces down on the table like that.'

It'll take your child more than one emotion-focused teaching moment to learn to label their emotions. Talking about emotions is an ongoing conversation, but one you can integrate into your day-to-day interactions. If you find it hard to remember to do this, look for emotion-focused books and toys that will help prompt conversations about feelings. The *When I'm Feeling* series by Tracey Moroney is a great set of books, but there are many great books about emotions for kids of all ages. For school-aged kids, the movie *Inside Out*, about a young girl and the five emotions (joy, sadness, anger, fear and disgust) that influence her life, is a great one to watch.

What to do when your child's in the red

Once your child hits red there's not a lot you can do. Your child's level of distress means a logical conversation of any kind is out, and persisting with reason-based strategies — problem solving, glass-half-full thinking — will only make things worse. As inadequate as it might seem, when your child's in the red, waiting out their distress is the main strategy at your disposal, but you can speed things up by diverting their attention. The more your child thinks about whatever it is that's driving their distress, the more upset they'll feel, and the faster things will spiral out of control. Taking a break from thinking about the problem at hand, at least for a little while, will help your child move back towards yellow.

When you sense a full-blown meltdown is on the horizon, get your child to their calm zone. This is an area your child can head to when they need to calm down. It can be anywhere in your house; the main priority is making sure that in their calm zone, your child has access to a range of activities they can use to cool off. Any activity is fine, so long as it's a calming activity and not one that's likely to cause too much excitement or intensify distress. Good calm zone activities for littlies are things like storybooks, music, puzzles, Duplo or colouring books. Younger and older kids can use these calm zone activities as well, but might also like drawing pads, sticker books, crosswords, arts and craft activities, Lego, or more physical activities like throwing a ball against a wall or practising basketball skills. Soothing activities like listening to calm music; hugging a pillow, soft toy or pet; watching glitter in a glitter jar; squeezing playdough or a stress ball, and muscle relaxation exercises are all good examples as well. If your child has meltdowns in public places, have a calm zone backpack as well as an allocated area at home, so your child can still access calm-down activities when you're on the go.

Explain to your child that as part of you helping them to be green, when you see them starting to lose control you're going to say something like, 'I think you're starting to go into red. Let's stop and calm down.' Go with your child to their calm zone and help them get started on a calm zone activity. When you first start practising, stay with them there until they calm down, and if they're able to use calm zone activities to reduce their distress, reinforce this with lots of praise and positive encouragement — 'I'm so proud of you for using your calm zone so well.' As your child gets better at using their calm zone, you can gradually remove yourself from the process by leaving your child for short blocks of time (a few minutes, five at most at first) and gradually increase the length of time between check-ins. How quickly you remove yourself will depend on your child, but as a general rule, if your child's younger or has more severe meltdowns, remove yourself from the process at a more gradual pace. Your child will still need your help getting started, no matter what their age, but with practice, eventually you'll be able to verbally prompt them to go to their calm zone without needing to physically prompt them as well.

Unless your child is exceptionally compliant, expect some push-back when you bring up their calm zone. Remember, your child is distressed and they're not thinking clearly. They need your help to build the skills they need to calm down, which means you keeping your cool as well. Instead of reacting to your child's resistance, roll with it. Validate your child's distress, reassure them that they're not in trouble, while gently persisting with encouraging calm zone activities. If your child's having trouble switching out of their problem-focused mindset, give reassurance that you'll help them with whatever they need, but remind them that you'll both come up with better solutions if you calm down first. If you're still met with resistance even after this, refresh and repeat. Your child will follow your lead and eventually participate in calm zone activities, but only if you persist. Keep trying, and as your child starts to calm down, offer lots of praise and reinforcement for their good work.

There's a huge difference between using a calm down zone and time out, so try not to confuse the two. Both strategies are aimed at building self-regulation skills, but time out achieves this (in theory) by giving kids time to regain control and think about the impact of their behaviour, while a calm zone helps kids to practise using self-soothing and distraction-based activities to regulate their distress. You can probably tell I'm more than a little biased towards the latter. There's nothing wrong with time out, and for some kids it's a great strategy, but when tantrums are distress-based, a calm down zone is a better approach.

Think about what helps you to cope when you're distressed. Does sitting on a chair to think things through help any, or is going for a walk or listening to music a better strategy? If your child's tantrums are behaviour driven, time out may end up working for you, but if the meltdowns are the result of genuine distress, it won't. Worse, because you're not helping your child develop skills to cope, their tantrums are likely to continue and may even worsen. And while lots of people take issue with giving kids access to toys and activities in their calm down zone, worried about the potential risk for reinforcing poor behaviour, this is really only an issue if you make the mistake of using a calm down zone for a tantrum that's behavioural in nature. If you use it correctly and at the right time, a calm down zone will help your child build the skills they need to manage their distress, so try it before you write it off.

Helping your child when they're yellow

Catching your child when they're yellow is key to helping them develop their emotion regulation skills. Once your child hits red, all bets are off. When they're yellow, yes they're still emotional and frustrated, but not to the extent that they've lost access to rational thought, making it an ideal time for skills practice.

The yellow zone is a small window of opportunity, so vigilance is essential. Know your child's yellow signs inside out and back to front, and when you see them, jump to action. Help your child practise emotion-focused skills like the ones below *before* they hit red.

Teach your child to talk about their feelings

If your child can't use words to share their feelings, they'll express their emotions behaviourally instead. Having the right words won't necessarily stop your child's tantrums all together but it should help to lessen their intensity and stop your child getting ambushed by their emotions.

If your child starts to show signs of distress, stop what you're doing. Give them your full attention — not half of your attention while you multitask, your full attention — and ask questions that will help you better understand why they're feeling frustrated and upset. Your child will be able to tell if you're going through the motions without any real interest, so try to be genuine in your desire to understand. When your child starts to talk, listen, empathize with their distress, and help them find the words to describe how they're feeling. Younger kids might have a hard time using words to talk about how they feel, so step in and help where you need to — 'I wonder if maybe you're feeling upset because I said I can't play with you right now' — but as your child starts to find their words, try to ask more questions than you answer. Being able to express feelings verbally without prompting will help your child develop the skills they need longer term, and your child needs the opportunity to practise. And no matter how ridiculous you think your child's reaction is, don't be dismissive of how they feel. Laughing at your child or making light of their feelings won't help; if anything, it's likely to make things worse.

It will be tempting to jump in with possible solutions to your child's distress; don't. Problem solving will come later but it's not the current objective. Before your child can start to think of possible solutions, they need to understand their feelings, and to have the headspace they need for this they need to feel heard and understood. Skipping ahead won't get you to your end goal faster — it'll probably slow you down. Take the time to listen to your child and validate how they feel before you start on any further skills practice.

Help your child practise mindfulness

Mindfulness is derived from ancient Buddhist practices, but it's become pretty popular in recent years, due in large part to the huge body of research documenting its mental and physical health benefits. Theoretically, mindfulness is simple enough: it involves deliberately paying attention to the present moment, whether that be external-focused aspects of your present moment (what you can see, hear, taste, touch, or smell) or internal-focused aspects (your bodily sensations, thoughts and feelings) without judging these experiences. Simple, right? Except for the fact that our minds are easily distracted and have a habit of focusing on everything *but* the present, and kids' minds are no exception.

In theory, by encouraging a focus on the present, mindfulness can help us manage frustration and distress, but it's a pretty tricky skill to learn, and like any skill it takes practice. It also requires sustained attention, which is why it's not a skill that'll work for most littlies. Kids over five will be able to develop mindfulness skills with practice, but most young kids will find it hard to be mindful for longer than five to ten minutes, depending on the task, so avoid long, drawn out mindfulness practices with kids under eight.

Before you start practising mindfulness with your child, help them to understand what mindfulness is. Say something like:

" Mindfulness is something we can do to help us feel better when we feel sad, angry or frustrated. You can practise it anywhere — all you need is your attention. When you want to practise mindfulness, you just need to stop and focus on what's happening in your body and around you. You can choose to pay attention to your breathing, how your body feels, what you can see or hear, things you can smell or feel — anything you like, so long as you focus on what's happening right now.

Once your child understands the general idea, start practising. Aim to practise a few times each week, but remember quality over quantity. Brief, frequent practices will be far more effective than fewer, drawn out practices. And be patient. Mindfulness is a skill even adults struggle with. Expect to have to put in the hours before you see any real results.

Mindfulness practice

Any activity can be used to practise mindfulness so long as deliberately staying focused on the activity is the priority. Your child might develop favourites, but try to keep mindfulness interesting by using a mix of tasks. Here are some ideas.

Smiling Mind. Smiling Mind is a not-for-profit Australian organization. They've created a free app — called Smiling Mind — with mindfulness programs for kids, teens and adults. There are 'bite sized' sessions of just a few minutes each, and longer sessions of fifteen or twenty minutes.

Mindful breathing. There are lots of different wants to practise mindful breathing. Blowing bubbles can help younger kids practise paying attention to their breathing, as can inflating and deflating balloons with slow, deliberate breaths. Older kids enjoy these activities too, but might prefer counting their breaths, counting 1 on the in-breath, 2 on the out-breath, etc. for ten breaths, or watching an object placed on their bellies rise and fall with their breath.

Mindful listening. You can encourage your child to practise mindful listening by asking them to name all the instruments they can hear in a piece of music, or to write out the lyrics in a section of a song they've never heard before (they can pause and rewind as many times as they like). They can also practise mindful listening anywhere by naming five sounds they can hear in the world around them.

Mindful looking. Mindful looking can be anything that encourages your child to focus on what they can see around them in the present moment — searching for bugs and insects in the garden, watching glitter fall in a glitter jar, searching for objects for each letter of the alphabet, following the path of a bubble until it pops or, for older kids, studying an object then trying to draw it from memory. If you want to make a glitter jar, you'll find lots of great recipes online.

Mindful activities. Any activity can be done mindfully, but activities that require your child to think and move will hold their attention more than tasks that don't require much movement, like watching TV or reading. Colouring in, puzzles, throwing a ball against the wall, or making bracelets out of beads are all good options for younger kids. For older kids, find-a-word puzzles, yoga or knitting are good options. And a general tip: asking your child to tell you what they're doing as they're doing it is a good way to help them stay 'mindful' and focused on the task at hand.

Mindful guessing games. Fill a pillowcase with objects from around the house — toys, kitchen utensils, items from your home office. Blindfold your child and have them pick an object from the pillowcase and guess, using only their sense of touch, what the object is. Ask them to describe what they can feel and talk you through their process of elimination. As your child learns how to play, try using objects that will be harder to identify. You can play a similar game with sounds. Use various objects around the house to produce sounds, and have your child guess, using only their listening skills, what object is making the sound.

Encourage your child to ask for help

When kids are upset or frustrated, they give up easily and default to an 'I can't' mindset, neither of which is particularly helpful. To break this cycle, your child needs to learn a new default: asking for help. When your child shows signs of distress, intervene. After listening to what your child has to say about how they're feeling and why, ask if they'd like your help. Model how to ask for help — 'If you're ever feeling frustrated because you can't do something, you can always say "can you help me?" and I will come and help you' — then help your child with whatever it is they're struggling with. Keep in mind that if you're too directive and bossy when you help, your child will be reluctant to come to you again, so try to only offer as much help as your child actually needs.

You'll need to model how to ask for help quite a few times before your child gets the hang of things, even more so for younger kids. But as they get better at asking for help, move away from modelling and use prompts instead. For example, say 'Is there something you need to ask me?' and wait for them to ask for your help. If they need an extra prompt, say something like 'What have we been practising lately? What could you ask me for?' If that doesn't elicit a request for help, go back to modelling, but otherwise persist with prompting your child to ask for help, before gradually phasing this out as well.

Help your child find a solution

Emotions affect not just how your child feels, but how they think as well. When your child's upset and frustrated, their thinking will be problem-focused and they'll find it hard to keep things in perspective. Their distress will trick them into thinking everything is worse than it actually is and that they have no control over the situation. But the truth is, most problems are solvable, even if only in part, and helping your child to adopt this mindset will go a long way towards helping them to keep their emotions in check.

When your child's upset, logical thinking will be a challenge, so be mindful of your approach. Timing will be key to your success, so don't jump in too soon with solutions and practical suggestions, because it'll only aggravate things. Take the time to ask your child questions to better understand their distress and validate how they feel, then once your child's relatively calm — and only then — start to work on helping them to adopt a solution-focused mindset.

Younger kids will need extra help initially to think of possible solutions, so put forward two or three and let your child choose which they'd like to run with. Don't put forward more than two or three solutions or your child will feel overwhelmed, and make sure the solutions you put forward are ones you're happy with. If you renege on the options you've put forward when your child picks the one solution you didn't really want them to pick, it won't end well.

As your child gets older, build their problem-solving skills by encouraging them to think of their own solutions. This may be a challenge if your child's distressed, so you may find that helping your child to practise problem-solving skills when they're in their green zone is a good first step. When your child's faced with a problem that gets the better of them, write the details on a piece of paper and put that piece of paper in a large jar — your new Problem Jar (shoe boxes work just as well). Later, when your child's calm, open the Problem Jar and practise brainstorming solutions for any problems you've stored away. As your child gets better at thinking of solutions to problems, try to encourage real-time problem-solving. Remember timing is everything, so you'll need to judge whether problem-solving is a viable option based on your child's level of distress, or whether you'll need to use other distraction-based strategies first, which will be the case if they're already in the red. As your child develops stronger problem-solving skills, they'll learn to adopt a solution-focused mindset when they're upset, and the option of solutions will help them to regulate their distress.

Not to be a broken record, but as your child gets older, remain conscious of how often you jump in with solutions versus giving your child the opportunity to think for themselves. That might be effective in the short-term insofar as it short-circuits their distress, but it won't help them develop skills to solve their own problems longer term, which will keep them stuck in their cycle of meltdowns. If you want your child to learn to solve their own problems and independently manage their distress, invest in teaching them the skills they need to do this.

Not all the solutions your child comes up with will be viable, especially early on, but when this happens, try not to be too discouraging. Feedback like, 'That's obviously not going to work — are you even trying?' will erode both your child's confidence and their motivation to practise problem-solving. Try instead to balance the need for corrective feedback with positive feedback and praise.

Let's say your child's had a meltdown because you asked them to turn off the iPad and do their homework. They didn't, so you've taken the iPad, and now all hell has broken loose.

" Parent: *(drawing on every ounce of patience they possess)* I can see you're really upset. What's going on?

Child: You took the iPad off me just as I got past a bit I've never gotten past before.

Parent: *(resists the urge to highlight that this isn't a big deal, and for effectiveness' sake, prioritizes understanding and empathy instead)* Okay, you were excited to finally get past the bit you always get stuck on, so it was a big deal for me to take the iPad away when I did. I get why you're frustrated.

Child: *(lets out a deep breath)*

Parent: *(noticing some of their child's frustration seems to have dissipated, decides to try problem solving)* Okay, well I haven't touched anything just yet, what should we do? You want to keep playing your game but you also need to do your homework; what's a good solution?

Child: I can finish my game now and do homework later?

Parent: *(knowing they need to balance constructive feedback with encouragement)* I like that you've come up with a solution, but I'm worried you'll be too tired for homework if we leave it to later. Is there another solution we can try?

Child: I'm not sure.

Parent: *(resisting the urge to jump in with a solution, which would rob the child of the opportunity to practise skills)* You're good at coming up with solutions. Give yourself a minute or two to think.

Child: Maybe I can pause the game, and if I do my homework now, I can have more iPad time after that? I don't have much homework.

Parent: Sounds like a good plan. Remember, screens have to go away by 5.30 p.m. and it's 4.15 p.m. now, so you'll need to focus and get your spelling done quickly. If you do, you'll have time to do homework and have extra time on your game.

Child: Okay.

Of course, real-life children aren't ever as compliant and reasonable as fictional ones, but you get the general idea. Empathise with your child's distress, wait until it's subsided, then encourage problem-solving skills practice.

Teach your child to be a glass-half-full thinker

How your child thinks about and interprets events has a huge effect on how well they manage their emotions. The ability to self-regulate goes hand in hand with the ability to adopt a reasonable, solution-focused mindset. Tantrums and meltdowns, on the other hand, are driven by negative, worst-case-scenario thinking, but also *cause* negatively biased, catastrophic thinking, too, creating a self-perpetuating, escalating spiral of distress.

Because your child's thoughts play such a big role in determining their emotional responses, skills for managing unhelpful thoughts are an essential part of their emotion regulation toolkit, especially once they're a little older. But trying to think rationally in the midst of huge emotion is a difficult skill for kids to master; they'll need lots of help and practice, so be patient. Encourage skills practice regularly, but don't expect to see results immediately.

When your child's upset or frustrated, encourage them to play the bad news/good news game:

> The bad news is I've got lots of homework, but the good news is if I get my homework done tonight, I can have a homework-free afternoon tomorrow.
>
> The bad news is my friend is sick and can't come over to play, but the good news is Dad said he'll take me to the park instead and I'm allowed to have my friend over next weekend.
>
> The bad news is I didn't do very well on my maths test, but the good news is Mum and Dad said they're proud of me for trying my best, and I know how I can improve next time.
>
> The bad news is I was talking in class and got in trouble from my teacher, but the good news is she accepted my apology and I don't have to stay in at lunch.
>
> The bad news is I'm too sick to go to my friend's birthday party, but the good news is I get to eat popcorn and watch movies in the lounge with Mum instead.

Practise the good news/bad news game most when your child is yellow, and use fictional scenarios or situations affecting other people to help them practise in their green zone as well. The more practice you give your child, the faster their skill development will be.

Note that kids younger than seven will be too young to use this strategy, but you can lay the groundwork for later skills practice now by modelling glass-half-full thinking. When you find yourself in a frustrating or upsetting situation, so long as it's a child-appropriate situation, show your child how to reframe it. For example, 'Argh, I'm so annoyed that it's raining today and we can't go to the beach like we'd planned. Oh well, the good news is it's good cookie-making weather, and we can go to the beach tomorrow instead.' The more you model glass-half-full thinking, the more likely your child is to adopt this way of thinking, so set yourself the task of finding the silver lining on a regular basis. As an added benefit, you may find it's a strategy that helps *you* to feel happier and less upset and frustrated as well.

Help your child make things right

When kids are learning to manage their feelings, they act impulsively, in ways they otherwise wouldn't, and as their distress starts to subside, regret, shame and guilt kick in, adding to their already fragile emotional state. Your child might know how to cope with frustration and general distress, but unless they're taught how to cope with complex feelings like shame and guilt, odds are they'll continue to beat themselves up when they make mistakes, increasing their vulnerability for additional tantrums.

If guilt and shame are tied up in your child's tantrums, teach him or her how to make things right. Encourage your child to apologize if their behaviour has caused harm or distress to someone else, and if their behaviour led to the destruction of another child's property (albeit accidentally) help your child make this right by organising a replacement. If your child's around ten years or older, make them partly responsible for the funds for this. Offer to pay for half, but ask your child to complete household chores to earn enough money to make up the rest. If your child's actions have hurt a friend, encourage more than an apology. Suggest they make a card or do something nice for their friend to show them how sorry they are.

Once your child has made amends, help them let go of their guilt. Tell them that everyone makes mistakes, even adults, and that it's okay to make mistakes, so long as we own up to our mistakes and do what we can to make things right. Praise your child for taking responsibility for their mistake and doing what they could to make amends, and let them know that now it's time to forget what happened because it's made up for and in the past.

Encouraging skills practice

You might think practising emotion regulation skills is a great idea, but don't be surprised if your child doesn't.

If you're having difficulty engaging your child in the process, bring a rewards-based system into play. How to use rewards effectively has been covered in detail already in Chapter 1, but remember that to be effective, the rewards need to be relatively immediate and meaningful enough to inspire your child to practise skills on an ongoing basis. If the rewards aren't appealing, they won't work, so think through your approach to rewards carefully and if you're struggling for inspiration, ask your child — they'll be only too happy to help you think of things they want.

Once your child starts to get the hang of how to manage their emotions, they'll need less encouragement to do so and you can gradually phase out tangible rewards. For effectiveness' sake, you'll still need to give verbal praise to reinforce positive behaviour, but you shouldn't need to keep using rewards on an ongoing basis. Just make sure you don't phase rewards out too quickly. Changing from a 1:1 goal behaviour to reward ratio to nothing overnight might cause a slight rebound effect, so when you're ready to start phasing out rewards, start a rewards chart for skills practice instead and use this to make the transition a more gradual one. (See Chapter 1 for how to use a rewards chart correctly.)

If your child's having difficulty managing big feelings across multiple domains — at school, during sports practice, at other people's houses — have a plan for practising skills in these environments as well. If your littlie attends day care or preschool, explain what you're trying to implement at home and see if staff can reinforce skills practice when your child's in their care. The same goes if your child is at school, and for any other adults involved in their life: parents who live separately, grandparents or other family members, coaches, family friends, etc. The more your child practises their skills, the better your chances of success, so look for opportunities to encourage skills practice in as many situations as you can, and reinforce this extra practice with praise and rewards at home.

When things don't go to plan

If your child doesn't seem to be responding to skills practice, make sure you're reading their level of distress correctly. If you misjudge things — if you think your child's in their yellow zone, but they're actually red, for example — you'll use the wrong strategies and your child won't be able to self-regulate, not because the strategies you're using don't work, but because you're using them at the wrong time. Go back and review your child's yellow and red warning signs, and see if you can catch their distress earlier.

How well you keep your cool when your child's distressed will also affect your success. Your child will take their lead from you, so if you're frustrated and upset, they'll stay frustrated and upset. Not reacting to tantrums can be hard, but the calmer you are, the faster your child will calm down. When your child starts to lose it, resist the urge to scream, and take a deep breath. Count to five, *then* respond.

Lastly, if you're not seeing progress, look at how often you're giving your child opportunities to practise. Practising skills at least two to three times per week is ideal. One to two times per week is okay, but any less frequently and your child will struggle to make much progress. Monitor the frequency of your skills practice, then increase it. Remember, the more you practise, the more likely you are to see results, so make practice a priority.

The important bits

+ Regular emotion-based tantrums are a sign your child needs help developing emotion regulation skills.

+ Your child is still developing the neural circuitry they need to self-regulate, but thanks to the plasticity of their brain, they can build regulatory skills through repetition and practice.

+ Your child's too young to work on skills independently, so skills practice needs to be parent-driven.

+ The situations that trigger your child's distress may seem silly to you, but dismissing their feelings isn't helpful. Have empathy for your child's struggles and try to see things from their point of view.

+ Once your child's in the midst of a full-blown meltdown, all bets are off. To teach skills for managing emotion, you need to know your child's early warning signs so you can catch their distress early.

+ Timing and strategy choice are key to you teaching skills for emotion regulation effectively, so be clear on what your child's early warning signs are and know which strategies to use when.

+ If trouble managing big emotions is what's behind your child's tantrums, getting distracted by poor behaviour won't help you to be effective. Prioritize skills practice so your child develops the skills to manage things better next time.

+ Teaching skills takes time, planning, effort and patience on your part but it's also what will help to stop your child's tantrums in their tracks. Persevere and you'll be rewarded with a happier, less temperamental child.

3

WHEN YOUR CHILD NEEDS HELP WITH FRIENDSHIPS

In the first two years of your child's life, social relationships are fairly contained. Most of your child's time is spent with family and close family friends, and while time with same-aged peers happens regularly too, these relationships aren't really what you'd call proper friendships just yet.

When your child enters their toddler years, though, things start to change. Other kids start to draw their interest, and play-based friendships become an important part of their social world. Fast forward to when your child starts school, and things change again. Play-based relationships develop into genuine friendships, and your child's desire for time with friends shifts alongside this. You're still high on your child's list of favourite people but friendships are important now, too, and time with friends is a priority in a way it hasn't been before. The drop from pole position can be a rough one, but try to think of it like this: your child is self-assured enough to seek out new relationships and that's not a bad thing — it's a sign you're doing your job well.

As your child's social world opens up, so will their exposure to playground challenges. Making friends and joining play for starters, but after that, other challenges come into play — ironing out disagreements over who's better friends with who and who wants to play what, coping with unnecessary nastiness and social exclusion, and finding solutions for hard-to-navigate social dilemmas, like what to do when your two best friends decide they don't like each other anymore. And then there's the challenge every parent dreads, one that affects far too many kids: bullying. A study examining the prevalence of covert bullying in Australia found that one in four kids aged between eight and fourteen has been the victim of bullying.[1] And, according to a recently released report by UNICEF, worldwide, the picture isn't much better. Bullying estimates vary greatly across studies, as do the average ages of participants, but the report labels Australia, New Zealand, the United Kingdom and the United States as medium risk countries, with monthly bullying affecting 42, 45, 27 and 37 per cent of young people respectively.

As frightening as issues like bullying are, it's not all bad. As your child's social world starts to grow, so will their confidence. Not only that, but because friendships provide your child with an opportunity to practise skills like sharing, cooperation and conflict resolution, as their social world grows their social skillset evolves and develops as well, helping to improve and strengthen their existing relationships and offering protection against social and emotional problems later in life. But, like any developmental skill, some kids need more help with friendship skills than others. Some because they've made friends with kids who aren't all that easy to be friends with, and others because they've struggled to learn the skills to make and keep friends. It doesn't mean your child's weird or unlikeable, or that they'll have issues with relationships throughout their adult life; they just need a bit of extra help to learn the skills to grow and develop friendships.

Help your child develop friendship skills

There's a lot you can do to help your child develop the skills to make and keep friends. Practice is key, so dust off your acting skills and get into a few role plays, and as your child's skills develop, prompt skills practice with same-aged peers as well. Which skills you work on will depend on your child's age and their current skillset, but the six skills your child needs most for making friends are covered below. Your child might need help across all six areas, or they might have strong skills in some domains but not others; if that's the case, look at which skills they need most help with and start there. If your child needs help with multiple skills, make sure you're methodical in your approach. Pick one or two skills to start (stick to one if your child is ten or younger) and build and consolidate these skills before you move on.

Don't forget to reinforce your child's skills practice with lots of praise. Rewards as well if they're called for. Your child might be happy to practise skills, and if that's the case, great. But if they're not, or if they're having difficulty transitioning from skills practice with you to skills practice with peers, be open to introducing a skills practice rewards chart (see Chapter 1).

Friendship skill 1: being a good sharer

Sharing is an important social skill to teach your child from an early age. If your child's a good sharer, it'll be easier for them to make and keep friends, and their ability to be flexible will mean they're better equipped to use solutions like turn-taking to manage playground conflict as well. Sharing isn't a skill that comes naturally to lots of kids, so don't be disheartened when your little cherub refuses to give things up. But all's not lost. Your child can learn to share, they just need help to practise.

Encourage your child to share and take turns with you at home. For example, say 'Okay, it's my turn to race a car around the track now, then it will be your turn again,' or 'Let's take turns on the Xbox; I'll go first, then you have a turn,' making sure you give your child the opportunity to practise going first *and* having to wait to take their turn. But if sharing proves to be a hard task, break your practice into smaller steps. Practise in really short bursts to start — fifteen minutes, for example, or as small a chunk of time as is necessary to help your child cope. As your child's tolerance for sharing increases, gradually build to longer periods of sharing. If that's not enough, you can modify your turn-taking ratio in the short-term as well. Use a 2:1 or even a 3:1 turn-taking ratio, for example. As your child's turn-taking abilities improve, gradually work back towards a 1:1 ratio.

Whichever approach you use (and you might have to use both) make sure you go over the top with praise and positive attention when your child shares and take turns well, using specific praise — 'I love how well you're sharing, good job' — so they know exactly what they've done to impress you. And if you still have issues, use consequences. When your child refuses to share, remove the object they're unwilling to share for about ten to fifteen minutes for littlies, fifteen to 30 minutes for younger kids, and up to an hour for older children. Then try again. Yes, all hell will break loose when you do, but it's this distress that will make your child more motivated to share in the future.

Friendship skill 2: asking for what you want/ need — nicely

If your child doesn't know how to ask nicely for what they want, they'll rely on less appropriate means like grabbing, pushing or shoving to get their needs met, and that won't help them any in the friends' department. Equally problematic, if your child avoids asking for what they want altogether — maybe they're shy or lack confidence — they'll miss out on opportunities to play with new friends or be unable to ask for help when they need it.

Learning to ask for things nicely is a base-level social skill, and one even littlies can practise. When your child's language skills are still developing, it's easy to fall into the trap of asking for things on their behalf, but try to avoid this where you can. Same goes if your child has a quieter temperament and looks to you to speak for them; this might be the easier option now, but it'll create unhelpful patterns in the future. Instead, prompt your child to make their own requests and to ask for help when they need it. If your child needs you to, model how. Say, 'If you'd like a turn, you need to say, "Can I have a turn on the computer please?"' or 'If you need help, say "Can you help me please" and someone will help you.' As your child gets better at asserting themselves, gradually phase out your modelling and prompts.

Friendship skill 3: starting and maintaining conversations

If your child's going to thrive socially, they need to know how to start a conversation. Encourage your child to introduce themselves to others in social settings by smiling, making good eye contact, and in a clear voice saying, 'Hi. My name's Ben. What's your name?' If your child finds this difficult, help them to practise introducing themselves to you at home first. If things are still a little shaky, do extra practice in front of a mirror or with other family members before re-starting real-world practice with peers.

A casual introduction is often all that's needed for younger kids to start playing together, but if your child's older, they might need additional help to build skills for initiating talk and keeping a conversation going. If knowing what to talk about is where your child struggles, help them develop a list of go-to questions about school, sports or interests. If initiating conversation is the issue, make this your target and help your child practise asking specific, open-ended questions like 'What games do you like to play?', 'What activities do you do?' or 'What do you like to watch on TV'. Closed questions — questions that can be answered with a yes/no response (e.g. 'Do you play sport?') — tend to be conversational dead ends, so be especially mindful of encouraging open-ended exchanges over closed questioning.

Once your child has the hang of conversation openers, extend their skills by practising active listening skills like nodding, smiling, adding comments ('I like that show, too') and skills for asking related follow-up questions ('How long have you played basketball? What position do you play?'). Each skill is tricky in its own right, especially skills for follow-up questions, so work on each individually first, before bringing everything together.

There's a lot to learn, so practise skills one at a time, and keep practising the same skill until your child has it mastered. If starting conversations remains an issue even after lots of practice, look at whether anxiety is playing a role. There's every chance your child's difficulties *aren't* anxiety related, but if you're serious about getting to the bottom of things, it's worth exploring all possible contributing factors. See Chapter 6 for more information on anxiety in kids.

Friendship skill 4: knowing how to join in

Joining others to play might seem like a simple enough task, but there are more than a few minefields your child needs to avoid if they're going to be accepted by their peers. Grabbing toys, yelling or taking over and 'improving' the game with new rules, for example, are courses of actions that won't be well received, and they'll as good as guarantee your child's social exclusion in the future as well.

If your child's having trouble with inclusion, don't assume it's the fault of their classmates. Kids can be cruel so it's certainly possible your child's being deliberately excluded, but equally plausible is that your child's having difficulties because they lack the skills needed to join play without rubbing others the wrong way, and that's something they'll need your help to change. For younger kids, use toys and figurines to teach right versus wrong approaches to joining in — for example, 'Teddy here can see Tom and Emma playing a game he wants to join. What's the best way for him to join in?' For older kids, teach skills directly via role play. Act out specific scenarios and help your child to learn that if they want to play a game others are already playing, they need to wait for a break in the game, then suggest they say something like 'What are you playing? Can I play too?' If the response is positive, help your child to understand that if they want to play, they should follow the instructions they're given and join the game, not try to change the game or start telling others what to do. Your child will need your help to understand that if they want to make changes or play something different, they can set up their own game with a different group of friends, but if they want to play *this* game with this particular group of friends, unless they're asked for their input, they need to go along with the rules already in play.

There's a chance when your child asks to play, they'll be told they can't join in. Not necessarily because other kids are being mean, but for other legitimate reasons, like the game being limited to a set number of participants and already at capacity. In case this happens, help your child have a plan for how to handle negative responses. Teach your child that when they're told they can't join in, they can say 'Okay, maybe next time' and find something else to do; stay and watch the others play; ask another group of friends to play; or if none of those options is workable, quiet time in the library is one you can recommend as well.

Unless you're fairly sure your child's exclusion is deliberate and malicious, don't include 'tell the teacher' in your list of things your child can do if they're told they can't join a game. This approach might work for littlies, but once your child starts school it's not helpful for them to run to the teacher each time they can't join a game. Unnecessary snitching creates more problems than it solves and ultimately sets your child up to be excluded. Nobody likes a tattletale, and if your child earns themselves a reputation as one, other kids will avoid them in the playground to avoid the hassle of unnecessary involvement from teachers.

Friendship skill 5: how to lose well

Being a good loser is a skill your child will improve at as their emotion regulation skills develop, but even the most able child will struggle to tolerate losing if they've not had any practice. Making your home a competition-free zone or losing intentionally so your child always wins might help to protect them from short-term disappointment, but longer term it creates problems. When confronted with a loss, your child won't know how to cope, and their reaction will affect their friendships.

Help your child learn the skills needed to lose graciously by setting aside time each week to practise. Play competitive board games, ball games, card games and *don't let your child win*. If they win naturally, that's okay, but make sure they have practice at losing as well. If practice triggers signs of frustration and distress, praise your child for continuing to play even though they're not winning, and try to focus on other elements of the game, like funny answers that make everyone laugh or fluky shots, not just who's winning and losing. If that doesn't work, suggest that you take a break and finish the game later. This should help your child to keep their cool, but if things escalate, use the strategies covered in Chapter 2 to manage any meltdowns.

Another strategy that works quite well with older children, so long as they're not too distressed and past the point of thinking logically, involves challenging your child's beliefs about the importance of winning. When they're caught up in the moment, winning seems all important, but the reality is, losing won't stay a key issue for long. You can help your child to keep their losses in perspective by asking questions like: Will this still matter to you in a week? In a few days? Tomorrow? In a couple of hours? The answer will probably be no, in which case feeling upset now isn't a worthwhile use of time. If your child's adamant that their loss *will* still matter in the future, test their prediction. Ask them to rate out of ten how much their loss matters right now, and then ask them the same question a few days, a week and a fortnight later. Odds are the loss they thought would matter forever actually doesn't, but an experiment like this makes this lesson more powerful. Repeat the same experiment any time your child is distressed over a loss to help them see that sometimes the things we think are really important, actually don't stay important or matter that much in the long term.

Kids will learn more from what you do than what you say, so make sure you model being a good loser as well as a gracious winner. Any sore losing on your part will be copied by your child, so be mindful of little eyes and ears, and make sure the lessons you teach through your actions match the advice you impart with your words.

Friendship skill 6: being helpful and kind to others

We should teach kids to be kind and helpful because it's the right thing to do, but research also tells us that kids who are kind and thoughtful are more liked and accepted by their peers, making kindness an important skill to teach kids for their social development as well. Some kids will be naturally kind, generous and thoughtful; others won't. Thoughtfulness is a skill that, like any other, can be taught. It just takes practice.

For school-age kids, help your child to think of ways they can be helpful and kind to others in their day-to-day life. If your child plays sport, they could help their coach pack away the sports equipment after practice. If they get a bus to school, they could make an effort to smile and say good morning to the bus driver. They could share their pencils and stationery with classmates who may have forgotten theirs, offer to help a friend if they're having trouble with work in class, hug a friend who looks upset, say something nice to someone just because, make a card for a friend who's been unwell, or step in and stand up for someone who's being picked on by other kids.

Set your child the task of performing one act of kindness every day. At the end of each day, ask them to tell you what they did, and if they were successful in being kind to others, no matter how big or small their act, offer lots of praise and positive attention. If they forget to perform an act of kindness, don't make too big a deal of it; respond neutrally — 'It sounds like you had a really busy day today' — and task them with a specific kindness goal for the following day.

Littlies will have too much trouble remembering kindness goals, but you can still encourage kindness; you'll just need to be more direct in your approach. When an opportunity arises, use real-time kindness coaching and specific instructions, for example, 'I think Annie is upset because Tom knocked her tower over. Go and ask if she'd like help to build a new one.' As with older kids, give your littlie lots of praise and positive attention when they act kindly, making sure you use specific praise so your child knows exactly what they did that was so great: 'I'm so proud of you for helping Annie. That was really kind and helpful. Good job.'

If your child's still having issues making friends

If after practising these skills your child is still having trouble in their friendships, look at how you can support their relationships outside school. Organizing play dates and sleepovers is a great first step. Yes, your child spends lots of time with friends at school, but in much the same way that spending time with colleagues outside work turns professional relationships into friendships, spending time with friends outside school will help your child develop better friendships and a stronger sense of security in their relationships. For littlies, shorter, more structured play dates are the way to go, and you should stay close by in case you're needed. Same goes if your child struggles with self-regulation or has a history of friendship problems. If your child's older, be around, but as long as there's no serious conflict try to leave them to play independently and only intervene if you really need to.

Once your child starts school, shared interests are a pretty important building block in friendships, so if your child's really struggling to make friends at school, encourage them to get involved in extracurricular activities like sports, music or drama. If the opportunity for extracurricular activities at your child's school is limited, do a bit of research to find out what activities other kids are doing outside school, and enrol your child in one or two of those. Likewise, find out (by asking your child or talking to their teacher) what games get played at break time, and if your child lacks the skills they need to get involved, help them to practise these as well.

And a quick note on electronic interests like video games. You might see video games as unnecessary and toxic, but odds are they're something your child's going to be interested in, even more so if their friends spend recess and lunch bonding over game-related tips, tricks and cheats. With everything that's been written about gaming addiction and the negative impact of electronics, it makes sense that your instinct will be to ban video games altogether (especially games like Fortnite) but before you do, pause to consider whether doing so might make it hard for your child in the playground. I'm not suggesting you give your child unlimited access to electronics or a gaming free pass, but the reality is kids, and boys in particular, bond over games and if your child can't contribute to these conversations because they're not allowed to play, they'll be on the outer. You might decide that, even knowing the social consequences, you still feel that gaming isn't the answer and not something you want your child to be a part of, and that's okay, you're the parent and you need to trust your judgment, but be open to at least considering your child's point of view before you do.

When your child's struggling with playground run-ins

Skills for making friends is one thing, but your child also needs skills for maintaining friendships and resolving conflict. Kids can be inconsiderate and uncharitable — some deliberately, others out of sheer thoughtlessness — so playground run-ins will unfortunately be a reasonably regular occurrence. If your child doesn't know how to handle conflict, they won't know what to do when disagreements arise, and their friendships will suffer, along with their confidence.

It will be upsetting to hear your child talk about any nastiness they've been subjected to by other kids, and your distress may well compel you to take matters into your own hands. Don't. Before you act, pause and take stock.

Ask questions to help you better understand exactly what's happened, making sure you ask questions like 'What did you do/say before he did/ said that?' so you can gauge if your child has contributed to the upsetting events in any way. Don't rely on direct questions like 'Are you to blame for any of what happened?' to get you this information because it won't work. Kids are self-focused thinkers and, without any malicious intent, your child will give you a biased, victim-focused account of events.

As your child describes what happened to upset them, repeat what you've heard so your child can correct any misunderstandings on your part, and as you do, try to stay calm. If you let your emotions get the better of you, your child might feel as if they can't talk to you when things go wrong — either because they misinterpret your reaction and assume you're mad at something they've done, or because they don't like to see you upset — and they won't come to you for help in future. Don't get too caught up in your own distress. Make your child's needs your focus.

When you have a better understanding of what's happened, show your child you understand by empathizing with their distress. Don't try to show you understand by recounting stories from your own childhood; well-meant as they may be, they'll frustrate your child and make them feel like you're making everything about you. Say something like 'I bet it was really hurtful and upsetting to hear Peter say that, especially when

Alex had just told you that you couldn't play. It's not a nice feeling when people say things like that. I'm sorry you've had such a rough day.'

Once your child has had an opportunity to vent and talk about how they feel, look at ways to help. One option is to get involved, but don't automatically jump to this. Resolving issues on your child's behalf might help solve things this time, but what about next time? Teaching your child skills to navigate social issues independently will mean they'll feel able to cope in any social situation, no matter what gets thrown their way, so make skills practice your go-to instead.

There are two skills in particular your child needs in their conflict resolution toolbox: assertiveness skills and social problem-solving skills. As with all social skills, practice is key, so don't just tell your child what to do: show them.

Assertiveness skills

Encouraging your child to stand up for themselves is a start towards boosting their social resilience, but you'll also need to teach them what being assertive actually means.

If your child's school-aged, start by explaining that people generally fall into one of three communication categories: passive communicators, aggressive communicators, or assertive communicators. Alternatively, use animal metaphors. For example, passive communicators speak quietly with poor eye contact, don't like to say no and have trouble standing up for themselves so as to avoid conflict — like turtles, who retreat into their shells when they feel scared or unsafe; aggressive communicators stand over people, speak in a loud voice, think their own thoughts and feelings are more important than anyone else's, and can be scary like an angry alligator; assertive communicators say what they think in a straightforward, non-threatening, respectful way, using good eye contact and a confident, calm voice, and they're equally respectful of their own thoughts and feelings and the thoughts and feelings of others — like dogs.

Use role plays to show your child what each communication style looks like in practice. Pick a few specific scenarios (some examples are listed below) and ask your child to help you act out passive, aggressive, and assertive responses for each, making sure you exaggerate actions so the differences between each communication style are clear. As you practise, note which communication style your child is best at because that's probably their default communication style. If they're more naturally inclined towards passive or aggressive communication, don't panic; you can help them practise being assertive.

Role play skills practice

Here are a couple of practice role play ideas. However, role plays are generally most effective when they resemble the scenarios your child is likely to have direct experience with, so use your knowledge of past playground struggles to make up your own role plays as well.

Scenario 1. You're playing with two friends and they start whispering behind their hands. You ask them what they're talking about but they won't tell you. What can you do?

- Example passive response: Keep sitting there while they whisper to each other and don't say anything else about it.
- Example aggressive response: Walk over to them and rip their hands down to stop them whispering, and yell at them for being rude.
- Example assertive response: In a clear, calm voice with good eye contact, say, 'I don't like that you're whispering to each other and leaving me out. It's making me feel upset and I'd like you to stop.'

Scenario 2. Your friends are playing handball but one of the boys is cheating and won't sit out even though he lost. What can you do?

- Example passive response: Say nothing and let him keep playing even though it means someone else will miss out on a turn.
- Example aggressive response: Walk up to the boy and push him out of his square. Yell at him to get lost.
- Example assertive response: Clearly and calmly say, 'Max, you got out, we all saw it. You need to go to the end of the line so other people can have their turn.'

If your child finds it hard to be assertive, help them to practise in front of a mirror (videoing practice works just as well) so they can see what they need to do to be more decisive and self-assured in their communication. Have them practise assertive phrases like 'I don't like it when you say nasty things like that, I'd like you to stop calling me names' or 'I don't understand why I can't play, let's find a way for me to be part of the game', so your child has an assertive repertoire to draw on. If they still need more help, you can shape their assertiveness with constructive feedback, but make sure you balance constructive criticism with positive feedback: 'You did such a good job that time using a clear, firm voice! Let's practise one more time and this time try to look me in the eyes while you say it as well. You're doing so well.' Limit yourself to one or two key suggestions, so your child doesn't feel dejected and overwhelmed.

You'll need to help your child practise being assertive on a regular basis. Coach your child and show them how to be assertive. If you see your child acting non-assertively in a social situation, pull them aside quietly and help them to plan a more assertive response. Similarly, if your child's upset about something that happened at school, get a blow-by-blow description of what happened, help your child to reflect on whether their response was passive, aggressive or assertive, and if it was a passive or aggressive response ask them to help you role play an assertive response so they know what to do next time.

If your child is five or under, or at school but struggling to grasp the difference between passive, aggressive and assertive communication styles, use more basic descriptions. For example, explain that some people are angry alligators and yell and shout a lot, some people are shy turtles and find other people scary, and other people are confident dogs who stand up for themselves but are still nice to others at the same time. When your littlie acts like an angry alligator or a shy turtle, pull them aside and help them change their approach. You'll need to be fairly directive, so don't ask what they could do differently; tell them what they should do instead. For example, say, 'I can see you're being an angry alligator because Sally won't let you have a turn with the skipping rope. Let's practise being a confident dog instead. Go and say "Can I have a turn with the skipping rope too?" and then wait for Sally to finish.'

Assertiveness is a tricky skill, so aim to practise a few times each week, remembering to offer lots of praise and positive reinforcement when your child's able to ditch their usual passiveness or aggression to respond with confidence instead. While you're teaching your child to be assertive, be mindful of how you communicate with others, too. Your actions are powerful. If your lessons on assertiveness are intermixed with demonstrations of passiveness or aggression on your part, your actions will overpower what you say, and your child will routinely react with passive or aggressive responses as a result.

If your child continues to react aggressively despite lots of practice and fairly good assertiveness skills, cast a wider net with your skills practice. Your child might have the assertiveness skills to respond effectively, but lack the necessary emotion regulation skills to keep their anger in check, and this might be why you're running into problems. Continue to practise assertiveness skills but add emotion regulation skills practice into the mix. A combined approach should help your child get back on track.

Social problem-solving skills

Your child will face all kinds of issues in the playground. Kids who refuse to play what your child wants to play, kids who are picky about who they 'let' play with them, and bossy kids who railroad play. Social problem-solving skills are a must to help navigate these issues. Kids younger than six or seven will struggle to learn problem-solving skills in full, so if your child's younger than this, stick to the age-related adjustments mentioned below.

When your child's upset about something that's happened at school, get a blow-by-blow description of what's occurred. Validate your child's feelings first, then once they're calm enough, ask them to help you brainstorm possible solutions to their problem. If they can't think of any ideas, suggest two or three solutions they can pick from, but only do this if your child actually needs you to. If your child's slow to think of solutions, it'll be tempting to jump in with your own, but try not to. Your child needs to learn to problem solve, and if you're too quick at jumping in with your own suggestions, you'll rob them of the opportunity to learn this skill. Instead, practise social problem-solving more regularly, using both hypothetical and real-life situations. With extra practice, your child will get better at solving their own problems — but only if you let them.

Once you have a list of possible solutions, look at the pros and cons of each, and ask your child to consider whether each solution will:

- help to solve their problem

- leave them feeling good about the way they handled themselves

- show themselves to others in a positive light.

If your child's seven or under, they'll struggle with evaluative thinking like this, so skip these questions and model pros and cons thinking instead so your child understands why certain solutions are better or worse than others. Once your child learns how to evaluate solutions, phase out modelling and revert to asking questions instead (e.g. 'If you skip hockey practice to go to Sally's house instead, what do you think your teammates will think? Can you remember what happened a few weeks ago when Melissa skipped practice to go to the mall? How did people react then?').

After you've looked at the pros and cons of each solution, rule out any solutions that won't solve your child's problem or are likely to cause further social issues — your child feeling bad about their actions or hurting someone else, for example — and ask them to choose the solution they think will work best. If their final solution isn't the one you would pick, resist the urge to take over (unless the idea is appalling) and let your child run with their own idea. Being more directive might lead to a faster resolution this time, but you'll also block your child from having the experiences needed to learn what works and what doesn't.

Use sibling squabbles to encourage conflict resolution skills practice

The list of things siblings fight about is long. Things like who gets to sit in the front seat, who gets to pick what to watch on TV, and whose turn it is on the iPad. And heaven forbid someone should borrow something without asking or look at someone the wrong way. Rest assured, sibling squabbles are pretty normal, and believe it or not, they actually have an upside: they give your child an opportunity to practise their conflict resolution skills. But only if you don't get in the way.

If you want your child to have the opportunity to practise conflict resolution skills, you need to limit how involved you get in sibling disagreements. Telling your kids you're not getting involved probably won't be enough, so establish clear household rules for conflict resolution instead. Make it clear to everyone that from now on, any instances of physical aggression or nastiness won't be tolerated, and if arguments escalate to the point where parent involvement is necessary, anyone involved in the conflict, no matter who said and did what and who started it, will be given a consequence for not having successfully and independently resolved the conflict. This sends a clear message that fights of any kind won't be tolerated, and your kids will be more motivated to resolve their conflicts independently, without you needing to get involved.

And because consequences are at play, it's best to bring rewards in as well. You can either take an individual approach, where each child is rewarded based on their own behaviour, or a team approach, where rewards are only up for grabs when both kids (or as many kids as there are involved) behave appropriately and resolve conflict well. Which approach you use will depend a little on the dynamic between your kids. If they are competitive by nature, in a positive way, an individual approach can work well. Keep in mind, though, that with an individual approach, if you don't directly witness the conflict resolution attempts, you potentially set yourself up for a he said/she said fiasco. If that starts happening, revert to a team approach. If your kids are competitive in a negative way — if rewarding only one child will trigger more conflict and create more problems — stick to a team approach.

With a team approach, the rewards and consequences you use will need to be meaningful to all kids involved. If your kids are similar ages and have similar interests, you'll get away with using the same rewards and consequences for everyone; but if they are different ages and have dissimilar interests, you'll need to have different rewards and consequences for each child. (See Chapter 1 for more on rewards and consequences.)

Do your best to make rewards and consequences comparable, but don't get drawn into arguments and negotiations over equity. Doing so will only reinforce feelings of entitlement and, worse, encourage the competitive comparisons you're trying to avoid. Ask each child for help — separately, and where age-appropriate — to establish their individual rewards and consequences, then should there be complaints later, remind your child that they helped to set their own rewards and consequences. If they still can't let it go, let them know you'll need to agree to disagree, and if the complaints continue, remind them that ongoing arguing won't be tolerated and you'll need to enforce a consequence if they're not able to stop.

The dos and don'ts of dealing with bullying

If the issues your child's having sound more like bullying than regular playground tiffs, take their concerns seriously. Bullying is a serious issue and if your child has had the courage to come to you for help, don't undermine their confidence in you by belittling their feelings. Don't interrupt with too many questions — there'll be plenty of time later to fine-tune your understanding of events — just let your child talk and give them your undivided attention. Reassure them they've done the right thing by coming to you — which will be a more convincing sell if you keep things neutral and aren't overly emotional in your response — and above all make sure your child understands that the bullying isn't their fault. Kids will often blame themselves for other kids' nastiness and your child needs to know that what's happened says far more about the bully than it does about them.

As you listen, keep a level head and don't jump to conclusions. There's every chance your child's giving you a complete description of events, but they might also be leaving out important details — not intentionally, but because they're feeling vulnerable and upset — leaving you with an only partially accurate run of events. Without all the details, you leave yourself open to making accusations you can't substantiate, and you might later discover your child's been more involved in the nastiness than they've let on. Don't rush in. Get your facts straight, then plan what to do next.

What is bullying

Bullying is any deliberate and ongoing, verbal, physical or social behaviour that's performed with the intention of causing physical, social and/or psychological harm. Isolated incidents, arguments between friends or one child not wanting to have a play date with another aren't bullying. Know what bullying is and what it isn't and don't trivialize its seriousness by using the term in contexts where it doesn't apply.

Some forms of bullying are obvious (e.g. physical bullying) but others are subtler, like social bullying, making it more difficult to identify.

Verbal bullying involves name calling; insults; teasing; verbal abuse; nasty remarks about someone's sexuality, race or religion.

Social bullying includes:

- spreading lies and rumours designed to harm someone's reputation
- making intimidating facial or physical gestures
- pranks or jokes aimed at embarrassing or humiliating someone
- mimicking someone in a nasty way
- encouraging others to socially exclude someone
- whispering designed to make someone feel left out.

Physical bullying involves hitting, kicking, shoving, pinching or causing physical hurt; damaging someone's property.

If your child's being bullied, it's likely they won't want you to contact their school in case it makes things worse. If bullying is happening on a regular basis or if it's physical in any way, let your child know that while you don't want to go against their wishes, it's your job to keep them safe, which is why you need to let their school know what's been going on. Try to give your child control where you can; let them decide, for example, whether they'd like you to speak to school on their behalf or if they'd like to be present for the discussion. But stick to your guns and speak to your child's school even if your child begs you not to. At the end of the day, your child's safety has to be the priority.

If bullying is happening semi occasionally and doesn't involve physical violence, and if your child wants to, give them the opportunity to fix things first — with your help. Even if school gets involved, they can't supervise every inch of the playground, and depending on their approach and commitment to ongoing monitoring, their intervention could unintentionally make things worse. Not only will teacher involvement not necessarily be the fix you think it will, relying on teachers also won't help to build your child's resilience against playground issues, which means if and when something like this happens again, they'll be just as vulnerable as they are now. Help your child to build the skills they need to cope, and if things don't improve within a few weeks, then call for reinforcements.

Help your child come up with strategies for what they can do when the bully takes aim. Bullies are often looking for a reaction, so acting with indifference and pretending not to care is usually pretty effective. Looking disinterested in the face of nasty remarks is a pretty hard task, though, so you'll need to help your child have plenty of practice. Start by asking your child to keep a straight face while you pull lots of funny faces and do your best to make them laugh. Once they've got the hang of that, help them practise looking bored and disinterested while you pretend to be the bully, but start with a reverse role play first: you play your child while your child plays the bully. Reversing roles means you can model how to act aloof and unbothered, but it also gives you the opportunity to learn more about the types of things the bully says, and this is key: the more realistic your role plays are, the more prepared your child will be in the playground.

Helping your child build a repertoire of go-to comebacks is another good approach, but be strategic. Encouraging your child to argue back or call the bully names in retaliation is a terrible idea. Any display of emotion will egg on the bully, so stick to comebacks that fit with a bored and disinterested approach, like, 'If you say so' or 'Really, that's interesting,' said in a detached, casual tone. Assertive responses can also work: 'I'm not really sure what your deal is, but this is getting a bit old. Aren't you bored yet?' Remember, the objective is to keep your child safe and stop the bullying; think ahead and make sure the advice you give you will help you to achieve that.

If you end up needing to get adults involved, unless you know the parents of the child your child has named as the bully really well (and I mean really, really well) don't go to them directly. Few parents respond well to being told their child's a bully, so the conversation won't go well. Go straight to your child's school instead. Leave it to them to investigate further and mediate a solution. Be prepared for the fact that your school will need more than 'My child says such and such is being mean to them' to take any action. Make a list of recent incidents, going into as much detail as you can, and if you know dates and times, include them. If there's been any online or phone-based bullying take screen shots of any abusive or nasty messages and include these as evidence. If the school still seems reluctant to get involved, try to keep your cool. Calmly let the school know you'd like them to take action, and organize a follow-up meeting in a week or two. Knowing there's an expectation of a response, and a deadline, should help to get things moving.

If you know the child's parents, you still need to plan your approach and choose your words wisely, regardless of how well you know them.

Avoid accusations, and try opening the conversation with a solution-focused statement like, 'I think my child and yours have been having some issues at school. I obviously only have my child's version of events, and that may or may not be the full story, but I was hoping we could put our heads together to try to get to the bottom of things.' Be open to the possibility that your child might have had a role to play in the conflict as well. Try not to get drawn into a he said/she said debate; keep focused on your objective — a solution that will help your child feel happy and safe at school.

If you're fairly sure — but not 100 per cent certain — you can have a productive conversation with the bully's parents, don't. Bullying is a sensitive issue that needs to be handled correctly, so think twice before you try to solve things yourself. If you have any doubts — any at all — talk to your child's classroom teacher to get their take on things, and go from there.

How will I know if my child is being bullied?

Not all kids who are being bullied will reach out for help. Some because they're embarrassed, others because they're afraid other people getting involved will only make things worse. Don't assume your child is the exception to this rule. Educate yourself about bullying and know the warning signs:

- mood swings or angry outbursts that are out of character
- changes to sleep and/or appetite

- recurring headaches or stomach aches
- unexplained bruises, scratches or cuts
- missing or damaged belongings (including clothing)
- change in attitude towards school (or an increased reluctance to go)
- drop in academic performance
- fear of going to school (including fear of travelling to school independently)
- withdrawing from friends
- not wanting to do usual activities.

If your child ticks one or two of these boxes, it doesn't necessarily mean they're being bullied. Many of these symptoms are non-specific and could be the result of any number of things. But if you start to see a pattern, or if your child ticks most of these boxes, talk to them. If they deny there's anything wrong, don't be put off, but definitely don't interrogate your child because it'll only make them more determined not to talk to you. Let your child know you're there to listen if they want to talk, and keep an eye on things. If things get worse or you have strong suspicions something's amiss, share your concerns with your child's teacher (including the list of symptoms you're seeing at home) and ask them to keep an eye on things for you.

What if my child's the one doing the bullying?

Being told your child's been bullying others is a hard pill to swallow. Accepting that it's true, even more so. But before you get defensive and go on the attack, pause and reflect. Your child's not a bad kid. They just need help to learn how to manage their frustration and navigate social relationships more effectively, and this is your opportunity to help them.

Start by having an open, honest conversation with your child about their actions. Let them know they're not in trouble, you just want to understand what's been happening so you can help. If your child won't open up to you or denies any wrongdoing, keep your cool. Odds are your child knows they've done the wrong thing and they're ashamed you know now, too. Don't get drawn into a debate over who said or did what, and definitely don't call your child a liar; focus on next steps instead.

Explain to your child that a complaint has been made, and that the school is taking it seriously. If your child blames their actions on those of another child (e.g. 'But he/she said or did something to me first') don't get distracted; let your child know that you know they probably did what they did for what seemed like a good reason at the time, but it doesn't make their actions right and it's never okay to bully others. If you think there's a chance your child genuinely doesn't understand what they've done wrong, give specific examples of their bullying behaviour so they know exactly what they need to stop doing (e.g. 'When you told Alex and Alicia yesterday that they couldn't play with Bronwyn, that wasn't okay'). Then help them to understand the impact of their actions — 'Bronwyn felt left out and it really hurt her feelings, and because you've pinched other girls in the past when they've not done what you said, Alex and Alicia felt too scared to not do what you told them to do. Making other people feel afraid isn't okay and it's not the way to make friends.'

Your overall goal is to help your child learn how to be a good friend, and to teach them the skills they need to rely on socially appropriate behaviour — not bullying behaviour — to get what they want. So, help your child practise the positive social skills outlined earlier in this chapter, along with skills for social problem solving and assertiveness. And if emotion regulation seems to be an issue, help your child learn how to manage their anger more appropriately as well (see Chapter 2).

Once you've got a skills practice plan, put a monitoring plan in place. Supervise play dates closely and give your child lots of praise and positive attention when they demonstrate positive social behaviours. If you witness any bullying behaviour or general nastiness, intervene and help your child use positive skills instead. And make sure you keep in regular contact with your child's school. Ask to be kept up to date with any incidents, and let your child's teacher know about your plan for improving social behaviour at home, so they can reinforce appropriate skills practice at school as well.

No one wants their child to have a reputation as a bully, and no one wants to be known as the parent of 'that child', but there's a right and a wrong way to go about things. Defensiveness won't get you anywhere; it'll make things worse. Be proactive and cooperative, do what you need to do to help your child change their behaviour, and you'll be surprised how quickly things get back on track. And if you're worried that your cooperativeness and willingness to acknowledge your child's wrongdoings will damage their self-esteem, don't be. If you offer lots of praise and encouragement for positive social behaviour, they'll know you're on their side, and your intervention will save them from years of friendship problems and potential social rejection. Your actions will help improve your child's self-esteem, not worsen it.

The important bits

+ As your child's social world grows, they'll need your help to learn social skills to build friendships and navigate playground challenges.
+ Verbal instruction alone won't help your child learn social skills, so help them practise social skills via role play and real-time coaching, and for best results, practise regularly and often.
+ Help your child practise the six key skills for making friends: being a good sharer; asking nicely for what they need/want; starting and maintaining conversations; joining in; being a good loser; being helpful and kind to others.
+ If your child's having trouble making friends, organize play dates, and help your child get involved in activities their peers are interested in.
+ Help your child develop conflict resolution skills, like assertive communication and social problem-solving skills for navigating playground challenges.
+ Be mindful of how involved you are in refereeing sibling disagreements; encourage your child to practise conflict resolution skills with their siblings instead.
+ When it comes to bullying, know the warning signs.

+ Help your child develop a plan for dealing with bullying so they feel more in control.
+ Don't approach other parents directly; go to the school instead, and don't make accusations you can't substantiate.
+ If your child's the bully, don't ignore or justify their behaviour. Help them to develop positive social skills instead.

4.

WHEN YOUR CHILD'S CONFIDENCE NEEDS A BOOST

Wanting your child to be confident is a no brainer. Confident kids are happy, outgoing and sociable, while their unconfident counterparts are insecure, shy and afraid to try new things, none of which are attributes high on any parent's priority list. In the younger years, building confidence is relatively easy: you make a fuss over newly learnt skills or small personal achievements, littlies feel a surge of pride, and their self-belief blossoms. But as kids start school and become more aware of how their skills and abilities stack up against their peers, building confidence becomes slightly harder. Personal accomplishments pack less of a punch, making an achievement-based approach to confidence building less effective than it has been in the past. So how do you build your child's confidence once they're old enough to understand the difference between average, better and best?

Protecting your child from failure and disappointment — by doing their school projects for them, taking the competition out of competitive sports, or only enrolling them in non-competitive extracurricular activities — isn't the right approach. Your child might feel better in the short-term when they get a good mark for their project or a ribbon for participation, but it won't build their confidence or add to their resilience, because their achievements aren't real — they've been orchestrated by you. If protection is your main go-to confidence-building strategy, you'll end up undermining your child's confidence, not strengthening it. Without meaning to, you'll teach them that achievement is important, so important that second-rate performances must be avoided at all cost, and that's not a helpful lesson for any child to learn, let alone one lacking confidence.

Whether in the playground, the classroom or on a sporting field, at one point or another your child will face challenges, failures and rejections that you can't control, and their confidence will only remain intact if they have the skills to cope. As backwards as it sounds, the best way to build your child's confidence is to acknowledge their weaknesses, not just their strengths, and teach them the skills to cope with failures and setbacks. Celebrating your child's strengths and the things they're good at can still be part of the equation, but other things also need to be part of the picture — helpful self-talk, feeling important in relationships, being competent and independent, and knowing how to cope with challenges and failure.

As your child gets older, a holistic approach is the key to building confidence. If you're worried that up until now you've been too focused on achievement or on protecting your child from failure and disappointment, don't panic. It's never too late to change your approach.

Plan your approach

There is a range of strategies you can use to develop your child's confidence. You won't necessarily need to use them all, and you definitely don't need to use them all at once. Building confidence is a balance game: so long as the things positively affecting your child's confidence outweigh the things negatively affecting it, their confidence should blossom. Consistency is also key, so stick to two or three strategies to start. Once you've focused on those two or three for a good length of time (between four and six weeks) switch things up and pick a different set of strategies to focus on.

Some kids develop confidence naturally and will need very little extra input from you. Others need more, but remember building confidence takes time. Unlike challenging behaviour (which, with the right strategies, is relatively quick to shift), building confidence is a slower process. Stick with it, and with perseverance and repetition, you'll see the progress you're hoping for.

Practical strategies for building confidence

The strategies are grouped into four sections below: achievement, feeling important, attitude and competence. Any and all of these strategies will boost your child's confidence, but as you're planning your approach, don't just target specific areas of vulnerability; try to balance your selection of strategies across all four sections. If you know your child struggles with failure or other achievement-based issues, for example, give more attention to strategies in this section (even if it means coming back to these strategies more than once) but also work on strategies from other sections. Don't get too caught up in perfecting your combination, because anything you do to build confidence is positive. Just use your parenting intuition and jump in.

Help your child have a balanced approach to achievement

Find things they're good at (and love to do)

Achievement and winning aren't great focuses to have, but there's no getting around the fact that being good at things is a confidence booster. So, help your child find activities they can excel at. If they pick up new skills easily, this will be a simple task, and your biggest challenge will be limiting their activities to a manageable few. But if your child doesn't take to new skills quite so well, don't give up. Keep trying different activities until you find the right one. It might take some time, but everyone has something they're good at, no matter what their skillset.

If you're struggling to find an activity your child's good at, look at whether you're trialling activities based on your child's interests, or whether you've fallen into the trap of pushing activities you want them to be interested in. If you push your own agenda despite your child's lack of interest, they're never going to excel, and you might end up making things worse. Get to know your child's interests and be guided by them.

If, on the other hand, your child finds an activity they love but they're not that great at, encourage it anyway. Praise them for their commitment and celebrate any progress. Yes, the goal might have been to find an activity they can excel at, but the ultimate goal is confidence. With the right support from you, participating in activities and interests your child loves and really enjoys will have the same effect, even if they're terrible.

Celebrate failure

One of your most important jobs as a parent is to help your child feel proud of their failures — no, seriously. If they see failure in a negative light, it'll hold them back. They won't want to try new things because the risk of failure will be too great, and when they do try new things and aren't as good as they'd like straight away, their confidence will take a hit. It'll take a hit, too, in any performance-based situation where your child doesn't perform as well as they would have liked: school tests and compulsory school sport tryouts, for example. They'll ignore the fact that they tried their best and didn't fail to try, and get stuck instead on their 'failure' and all the ways they find themselves lacking, all because they've learnt that failure is bad and something they should avoid at all costs.

Failure isn't something you should protect your child from. It's something you should encourage, because it's not a sign of incompetence or weakness; it's a sign of courage and strength, and an opportunity to learn. If you can teach your child to see failure this way, it will become one of their most valuable tools for success. So, when your child spends a lot of his basketball game benched because he's not as good as his peers, don't have a quiet word to the coach and demand he give your child more court time. Acknowledge that basketball isn't your child's biggest strength, which is okay because no one can be great at everything. Help him to practise and improve where he can, celebrate any wins along the way and praise his perseverance and willingness to have a go.

Teach your child to live courageously, to embrace failure, and to be proud that they didn't fail to try. Encouraging failure won't damage their self-esteem; it'll build their resilience and help to grow their confidence.

Help your child set PBs

Peer-based comparisons have the potential to undermine your child's confidence, especially if your child isn't as skilled as their same-aged peers. So when setting goals, encourage your child to set 'personal best' goals (PBs), not comparative goals. If they want to be better at maths, for example, look at how they're currently performing and set a goal that's a slight improvement on that. Likewise, if they want to be faster at running, don't encourage your child to have another child's time as their target goal; encourage them to focus on improving their own best time instead.

You'll need to help your child come up with a plan to achieve their new goal (e.g. extra study or practice) to increase their chance of success. But along the way, your main objective will be to keep your child focused on their own performance. That most school and extracurricular activities encourage peer-based comparisons makes this challenging, but it's worth persisting with your PB plan. If you can teach your child to focus on improving their own performance and to worry less about outperforming others, it'll go a long way towards building their confidence and protecting their self-esteem.

Make sure your child feels important

Listen when your child talks

Kids talk non-stop, and even though much of what your child says might seem trivial to you, it's important and meaningful to them. And so are you. You're so important, in fact, that when your child talks and you don't listen, it threatens their confidence. Think about how you feel when you try to talk to your partner and they can't tear their eyes away from a screen long enough to listen. It's frustrating, right? You're left feeling dismissed and unimportant, and that's exactly how your child feels when you tune them out.

When you actively listen, and give your child your *full* attention (not half your attention while you cook dinner/send an email/watch TV, your full attention) it makes them feel important and boosts their confidence. And when you show interest in what your child says by nodding, asking questions or practising empathy, they feel heard, supported and understood, and that also bolsters their confidence. So, when your child comes to you with what you think is a trivial issue or yet another extraneous piece of information, resist the urge to tell them you're busy and make time to listen instead. Don't undervalue the power of listening. Show your child they're worthwhile and important by being attentive to their chatter.

As your child heads into their pre-teen years, you can show you're really listening by letting go of your 'I make the decisions and you'll do what I say because I said so' parenting approach and switching to a collaborative parenting approach. (There's more advice on this in my book *Skip the Drama: Practical get-ahead strategies to survive your daughter's teenage years*.) As backwards as it sounds, when your child enters their pre-teen years and starts to develop their own thoughts and opinions, taking your child's feedback on board and collaborating on limit-setting will not only earn you their respect and give you a smoother run into the teenage years, it will make your child feel valued and respected, and when it comes to their confidence, that's powerful.

Make quality time a priority

One of the best things you can do to help your child feel good about themselves is spend time with them. When you don't make time for your child, it doesn't go unnoticed. Your child gets your 'You're not important/interesting/likeable enough for me to want to spend time with you' message loud and clear and it affects their confidence. It might not be the message you're meaning to send, or the one you want your child to have, but it's the one they hear all the same.

When you prioritize quality time with your child, it boosts their confidence. They feel loved and valued, and that makes them feel like a million bucks. You don't have to spend copious amounts of time with your child for it to have an impact. It's great if you have time to do a special activity with your child each week — go for a milkshake or breakfast together at the weekend, pick them up from school one afternoon a week to go bike riding or to kick a ball at the park. But if you don't, you can still show your child you think they're awesome by giving them short but regular bursts of your undivided attention. Set aside fifteen minutes each evening to sit and chat with your child about their day, spend fifteen minutes reading together before bed, or help them practise their ball skills in the yard for ten minutes or so a couple of times each week. How much effort you put into your relationship with your child will matter to them.

Encourage your child's friendships

Having friends and a sense of belonging will boost not just your child's confidence, but their resilience as well. And while the school playground offers an opportunity for your child's friendships to develop, spending time with friends outside school is equally important. After-school and weekend play dates make friendships stronger, and that translates to your child feeling more secure and confident at school, and in life in general.

If your child's struggling to make friends, work on the friendship skills covered in Chapter 3 before organizing any play dates. The issue may well be that your child's just unsure how to join in play, but if there are other issues (lagging conversational skills, issues with losing and sharing, being silly or deliberately annoying as a way to connect) play dates won't fix the issue. Help your child overcome whatever issues they're struggling with, and then work on increasing time with friends outside school.

Help your child have the right attitude

Encourage kind self-talk

How your child talks to themselves throughout the day has a huge impact on their confidence and self-esteem. Kind self-talk works to boost and protect confidence, while nasty self-talk damages it.

Because self-talk has such a big role to play when it comes to confidence, teaching your child to adopt kind self-talk is a strategy worth your time.

It's by no means a quick fix, so you'll need to be patient and prepared to put in the hard yards before you see any real results. Kids under seven might struggle to verbalize their self-talk, some because they can't find the right words, and others because they haven't yet developed awareness of their self-talk. If that's true of your child, hold off on this strategy for now. Model kind self-talk where you can, and when your child develops skills to talk about their thoughts, make a start on the strategies outlined below.

If your child's old enough, start by talking to them about self-talk. Explain that our brain thinks all day every day because that's what they've been built to do, and sometimes these thoughts are kind and helpful, but other times they're nasty and unhelpful. To help your child have a clear understanding of what you mean by kind and nasty thoughts, give them specific examples. For example, explain that if they were to miss a shot at basketball, nasty self-talk might sound like 'I'm such a loser', but kind self-talk could be 'That was really close. There's still lots of game time left. I bet I make the next one.' Likewise, if they were to score three out of ten on a spelling test, a nasty self-talk thought might be 'I'm stupid', whereas kind self-talk might be something like 'I made a couple of silly mistakes so I know I could have done better. I'll do more practice and I bet I do better on the next quiz.'

Catching nasty, or negative, thoughts is a tricky skill. Because nasty self-talk happens in the privacy for your child's head, it can be hard to find ways to help, but if your child's self-talk is negative, their words will be too, and that's what you need to look out for. When you hear your child berating themselves or being too self-critical, say something like, 'That sounds like one of those nasty self-talk thoughts to me.' If they tell you it's not a nasty thought, it's the truth, don't get drawn into a debate because it won't help you to be effective. Just say, 'What would happen if you said that to a friend in the playground?' Your child will know that if they said what they just said about themselves to a friend they'd get in trouble for being mean, and that's when you step in with a new self-talk rule: if you wouldn't say it to a friend, don't think it to yourself.

Explain to your child that, just as bullying isn't okay at school, self-bullying isn't okay either. Then help your child reframe their nasty self-talk into kind self-talk. If your child has trouble with this (which they probably will, at least to start) suggest that they think about what they'd say to a friend in the same situation. Thinking about things from this angle will make the task easier. And, with practice, their kind self-talk will happen more naturally.

Help your child cope with mistakes

Your child's going to make mistakes. Some will be small, like spilling food and drink on the living room rug. Others will be bigger, like being dishonest, being mean to someone they've decided they don't like, or not standing up for a friend. The mistakes they make won't in and of themselves be problematic, but they have the potential to be detrimental to confidence if your child sees them as permanent and unfixable. Whether they do depends a lot on the lessons they learn from you.

When mistakes happen, you're well within your rights to tell your child off for their gross negligence/appalling behaviour/poor decision making (especially if their mistake involves damage to property), but it won't help a great deal. Help your child to learn from their mistake and right their wrong, though, and things will work better all round. Your child will learn that they need to make better decisions in the future, and because they've done their best to make it right, their confidence will be more protected as well. And no, this doesn't mean your child gets off scot-free. They'll still feel the weight of their mistake, and you can still follow through with a consequence, but using only consequences isn't the way to go. Your child is a work in progress and they're going to make mistakes. Expecting otherwise is unrealistic, unhelpful and unfair. Don't expect perfection; teach your child how to make things right instead. Not only will you be a more effective teacher, you'll protect your relationship and help your child grow their resilience as well.

If your child admits to their mistake, don't let that go by unnoticed. Being able to admit to and take responsibility for mistakes is an important life skill, and one many adults haven't mastered yet. If your child has the ability to own up to their error in judgment, that's huge. Give credit where credit's due — no matter how irritated you are by the mistake itself — then move on to processing. Explain that everyone makes mistakes sometimes, and there's nothing wrong with that, so long as we learn from our mistakes and fix them where we can. Ask your child what they think they can learn from their mistake and encourage them to come up with ideas for how they can make things right, then sit tight and give them time to think on this.

Most wrongs can be set right: messes can be cleaned up, breaks can be fixed or objects replaced (at your child's expense) and hurtful actions can be forgiven with a thoughtful apology, so don't let your child give up. Persevere until there's a repair plan in place. If your child really struggles to come up with ideas, put forward a few of your own, but don't set this up as a permanent pattern. Offer suggestions while your child gets the hang of things, then step back and task them with coming up with their own ideas. If your child's really upset over their mistake, they'll find it hard to think clearly enough to brainstorm. Make reducing their distress your first target, and come back to your post-mistake review later.

Once your child has learnt their lesson and made amends, let it go. Going over old ground won't achieve anything, it'll just make your child feel bad. Worse, your reaction will teach your child that trying to make things right is pointless, because no matter what you do and how hard you try, people won't ever really forgive you, and that's not a message you want to send. Deal with mistakes one at the time, then move on.

Build your child's sense of competence

Give them responsibilities

Being entrusted with responsibilities makes kids feel important. It gives them a sense of pride and self-satisfaction, which is why giving your child a set of tasks to be responsible for is another good strategy for building confidence. Tasking your child with responsibilities from a young age offers you insurance against bratty and entitled behaviour in your child's teenage years as well — so get delegating.

Exactly which tasks you give your child will depend on their age, but even littlies can be given responsibilities like packing away toys, helping to take clothes out of the washing machine, or helping to unpack plastic items from the dishwasher. When your child starts school, other responsibilities like packing/unpacking school bags, making beds, putting away laundry, helping to unpack the groceries and clearing the table after dinner can be added into the mix. Too many responsibilities will overwhelm younger kids, so limit their jobs to two or three at most, keeping it to just one initially while they learn the ropes.

As your child gets older (from around ten, depending on your child) their responsibilities might grow from single to multitask responsibilities. For example, getting ready for school (having breakfast, brushing hair and teeth, getting dressed, packing a bag, getting shoes and socks on) or getting ready for bed (shower, pyjamas, teeth and toilet, reading, bed). When it comes to multitask responsibilities, some kids will find it easy to stay on task and remember what comes next; others will have a bit more trouble. If your child falls into the latter category, try writing their task list on a whiteboard and using coloured magnets to mark which tasks have been completed and which are still outstanding. If the whiteboard is small enough for your child to carry from room to room, that usually works best, but a reference board in your child's room will work well too. If your child still has trouble, try focusing on one routine to start, either their morning or evening routine, whichever you think they'll have the most success with. Then return to working on the other routine later. You can also try reducing the number of tasks your child's responsible for in either routine. Start with tasking them with just the first two tasks on their list, for example (you'll need to help them with the rest) and as they start to get the hang of things, add new tasks one at a time until they're successfully completing the full sequence of tasks independently.

If staying on task is an issue, you can also ask your child to describe out loud what they're doing as they're doing it. This should help them stay focused on the task at hand, but you'll still probably need to be in the same room as your child while they practise this, at least initially.

If so, try not to re-give instructions if your child gets off track, just give prompts like, 'What job are you supposed to be doing?' and only sparingly. The more prompts you give, the more reliant your child will be on these prompts, and you'll have a harder time phasing yourself out of the equation. As your child starts to manage independently, take a step back. Be in a different room while your child calls out what they're doing, then have them whisper their actions to themselves, before practising just saying their actions in their head. By this stage your child should be fairly competent at completing tasks independently. If you're still having difficulties with staying on task, approach the issue from a behavioural perspective, using the strategies covered in Chapter 1.

If your child has access to an iPad, there are quite a few good apps to help kids stay on task with their morning and evening routines. One I use a fair bit is called Happy Kids Timer, and it helps kids work through their morning and evening routines. The list of tasks your child needs to complete is fully customizable, and you can set a time limit for each to mitigate dawdling. If your child completes their tasks within their set timeframe, they're rewarded with a series of stars, which count towards the target number of stars needed to earn an agreed-on reward.

And while we're on rewards, as your child gets older, the novelty of being entrusted with responsibilities will start to wear off and as far as your child's concerned, high-fives and positive feedback won't cut it. If you're suddenly met with resistance, don't panic; introduce rewards instead (see Chapter 1). When your child hits their teenage years, you can rely on logical consequences to motivate action instead: only wash clothes if they make it to the dirty clothes basket, for example. But for right now, rewards are a better bet. Your child's still learning the skills needed to remember and act on their responsibilities, and so long as that's the case, logical consequences won't be effective. Rewards will help your child practise the skills they need for the future, so use them when you need to.

Teach your child to solve their own problems

When you take it upon yourself to solve your child's issues for them, it isn't helpful. If your child's not part of the problem-solving process, they won't know what to do or how to cope when they're faced with their next problem, or any of the problems they'll face after that. Having to rely on you for fixes undermines their confidence, because they'll start to believe they can't cope without you. On the other hand, having the skills to independently solve problems and the ability to find solutions to any problem any time will do wonders for their self-esteem. And it's achievable — it just comes down to practice. For more on problem solving, revisit 'Help your child find a solution' on p. 73 and 'Social problem-solving skills' on p. 101.

High emotion will mess with your child's ability to think logically, so don't practise problem solving when they're upset or frustrated. Help them manage their distress first (see Chapter 2) then revisit problem-solving skills practice later.

Let your child do things for themselves

Helping your child to master new skills and develop independence is an easy way to build their confidence. In littlies, this might mean stepping back a bit and letting them navigate the playground more independently or giving them the opportunity to get themselves dressed or butter their own toast. In older kids, mastery and independence can mean any number of things: giving your child tasks to complete in the kitchen, allowing them to walk to the school bus stop by themselves, encouraging them to order their own food in a restaurant, helping them to ask others (shop assistants, librarians, bus drivers) questions directly should they have any, or completing homework independently. Whatever the task and no matter how old your child is, the key is this: give suggestions or show your child what to do, then step back and only intervene if they actually need you to.

Letting your child do things for themselves might mean biting your tongue and sitting on your hands to stop yourself taking over, but the confidence your child gains from learning to do things on their own will make it worth it. Invest in teaching your child the skills they need to be self-sufficient now; it'll pay off longer term. If things get done less than perfectly — beds made crookedly, vegetables peeled a bit shoddily, or homework that's a bit messy — resist the urge to step in and fix things. Correcting your child's efforts will work against your goal of building their confidence, so before you intervene, ask yourself what's more important: perfectly completed tasks or your child's confidence?

Let your child make decisions

You can build your child's confidence by giving them some control. The best way to do this is to give them some decision-making power. Offer choices around meals, clothing, after-school activities, any area you can.

But be prepared to be okay with whatever decision your child makes or it defeats the purpose of the exercise. Say you tell your child they can pick what's for dinner and they suggest pizza. If you then tell them they can't have that and ask them to pick something else, this undercuts the feeling of control you're trying to create. Likewise, if your child gets themselves dressed, but you make them change because their shorts and top don't match, any satisfaction they might have felt at exercising their decision-making power will evaporate quickly, as will their confidence.

If there are limited options for your child to choose from, make this clear from the outset. Don't tell them they can choose any activity for you to do together if tennis, swimming or a board game are their only options. Be clear about what their options are, and ask them to choose from a shortlist of activities. And if too many options tend to overwhelm your child (this will often be the case with littlies or kids with anxious temperaments) deliberately narrow the choices on offer to two or three. This will make it easier for your child to make a decision and ensure that decision making helps rather than hinders their confidence.

On quitting

A lot of parents worry that if they let their child stop an activity, they'll learn that quitting is okay. To be fair, that probably will be the take-home lesson, but that's okay because deciding to quit something is okay.

If your child's been trying a new activity and they've given it a go for a few weeks, it's okay for them to quit if they don't like it, especially if the decision is a considered one and not one they've made reactively off the back of a negative event. Quitting the activity won't negatively impact their self-esteem. In fact, supporting your child in their decision will serve to boost their confidence, not harm it.

If the activity is a team sport or if there's a financial commitment involved, let your child know that because they've made a commitment to other people they'll need to see the season through, but after that it's entirely up to them whether they'd like to continue on or find another activity. If this gets their knickers in a twist or if your child really, really hates the activity, give them other options. Tell them they can forfeit their position on the team if they speak to their coach themselves and continue to play until the team finds a replacement, and if they agree to complete additional chores as repayment for the money you can't have refunded. So long as your child takes responsibility, does the right thing by others, and is an active participant in this process, quitting still won't negatively impact their confidence. They've independently made a decision and owned it, and that's a good thing.

Confidence building: what not to do

Don't tell your child they're good at things if they're not

There's no point telling your child they're terrific at everything because odds are, they're not; *no one's* good at everything. If you give too many pats on the back or compliment your child too freely, they'll know you're lying, and your praise (even praise that's genuine and accurate) will be dismissed. Alternatively, your child *won't* know you're lying and they'll come to believe they're far more skilled than they actually are, inflating their confidence and increasing their vulnerability for disappointment and public humiliation.

Your child needs to understand that there are things they're good at and things they're not so good at, and that's okay. So when you're child's not good at something, say something like, 'I know you find maths really hard. I'm really proud of you for trying and putting in so much extra work. There are lots of things you're good at: spelling, science, soccer, helping other people. And you're really good at telling time now, and your times tables, that's maths as well. It's okay not to be terrific at everything. Just keep trying and doing your best. That's all that really matters.' Be aware, though, that more insistent you are, the more it will seem like not being good at something is a really big deal, so keep things neutral and unemotional. The less of a deal it seems to you, the less it will matter to your child.

Don't set your child up to fail

Set clear, realistic expectations for your child. If you expect more of your child than they're able to give, it'll be frustrating for you both, an ongoing source of arguments, and you'll end up inadvertently undermining your child's confidence.

No matter how tough their exterior, your child desperately wants to please you and make you happy. When they can't meet your expectations, they feel bad, and when it happens on a regular basis their confidence takes a hit. Don't set expectations based on what you wish your child could do; set them based on your child's age and developmental skillset. Yes, it'd be a huge help and a win for your child's confidence if they could get themselves ready in the morning and manage their own homework, but that'll only happen if they have the skills they need to be successful. Likewise, yes, your child would probably feel really good about themselves if they managed an A at school, but if their ability is set at a B, an A isn't realistic, and if you continue pushing for one, it'll affect your child's confidence and discourage their efforts in the future.

What you think matters to your child. Set your child up for success, and watch their confidence flourish.

Don't be unkind

Between the strain of parenting financial pressures, marital problems and workplace conflict, life can get pretty stressful. When it does, it's easy to take your frustrations out on the people around you, especially your kids. But as understandable as your frustration is, if you don't have a handle on it, it can have repercussions for your child's confidence.

Your child worships the ground you walk on. They have a funny way of showing it sometimes, but it's true nonetheless. When you say things in anger, like 'What's wrong with you? Why don't you ever just do what you're told? Get out of my sight,' it packs a punch. Once your anger passes, *you* might know that you didn't mean what you said, but your child won't. Your words, and the vehemence with which you said them, will be etched in their memory, and if it happens regularly enough it'll make your child feel lousy and inadequate.

When you're under a lot of stress and your kids are getting on your nerves, take care of yourself — start back at the gym, develop an action plan for work, organize child-free time with your spouse — but don't take it out on your kids. Your child hasn't done anything wrong, and if they have, there's a right and a wrong way to go about things. Don't berate your child and don't speak to them in a nasty tone or intimidate them with your volume: 'You think you're funny don't you. Do you see anyone else laughing? Do you? No. Everyone else thinks you're a pain as well.' And don't compare them in a derogatory way to other kids: 'Why can't you be more like your friend Alex? He never acts like this.' It's not necessary, and it's not helpful. If you need to reprimand your child, use neutral language and let consequences do the talking for you. You'll have more success achieving the outcome you want, and your child's confidence will be protected as well.

How you speak to your child matters. Choose your words wisely.

If overconfidence is the issue

With some kids, overconfidence bordering on arrogance will be your parenting challenge. If your child starts rubbing other kids' noses in their excellence, take action. Rescaling your child's confidence will be a delicate task, but arrogance will make your child wildly unpopular with friends and classmates, and bragging isn't a skill you want to encourage.

How easy it is to change things will depend on the cause of your child's arrogance. For some kids, arrogance is actually a front for low confidence. If that's the case, building your child's confidence should help turn things around, and it should be a relatively easy fix if you follow the strategies outlined in this chapter. In other kids, arrogance is learnt, and that can be slightly trickier. Over-praise is the most likely culprit, so odds are it's your schedule of praise that needs to be rejigged. As a lot of recent research suggests, praising your child too much or without valid cause won't build confidence in a positive way. It'll breed arrogance and self-admiration, neither of which is particularly endearing. If you suspect you might have inadvertently over-stepped into unhelpful praise territory, scale things back a notch. Give praise only when it's warranted, and make *effort* rather than *achievement* your focus. It might take your child a while to respond to the new state of play, but they will in time, so keep at it.

If your child's a bit of a hot shot, this can have ramifications for their confidence as well — especially if they're good at lots of things — and this type of arrogance is usually harder to shift. In this instance, your child is overconfident because they have reason to be, but that won't make their arrogance any more palatable. The best way to deal with this is to help your child focus on being a good sport and a humble achiever. Teach your child that there's more to being the best than placing first and winning; how you win and how you treat others matters just as much, if not more.

When your child encourages others and is gracious in their wins, offer lots of praise, but be specific, so they know exactly why you're proud of them. When they're arrogant and disparaging towards others, call them out on it and help them change their behaviour. Exactly how far you take things will depend on their level of arrogance, but as a general rule, mild arrogance can probably be addressed by parent modelling and direct instructions (e.g. 'I know you played well and that helped your team win, but it was a team effort and you couldn't have scored the goals you did without your teammates. Go and shake everyone's hands and tell them they played a great game today.') More intense arrogance might need a more structured approach — specific behavioural goals with designated rewards and consequences, for example, much like the ones used by Peter and Lisa below.

Peter and Lisa's son Avery is a highly skilled football player. At just eleven years of age, he's already been selected to play for state and national teams. It's not just football he's good at: he's also earned a solid reputation as a track and field star. Academically, Avery performs in the top 5 per cent of the state and has aspirations to be a neurosurgeon. There's just one problem. Avery's good, and he knows it, and it's starting to affect his opportunities.

66 Avery used to be such a down-to-earth kid, I really don't know when his confidence started to become such a negative. He has every reason to be confident, he's popular and really good at school and sports, and I'm sure it doesn't help that people are always telling him what a star he is, us included. But we're worried he's getting a bit cocky. He's constantly bragging about how good he is, and even though it's true, it makes us cringe every time we hear it.

He used to just brag about things at home, but other people are starting to notice it, and they're not impressed. His teachers have told him to tone it down because his bragging is starting to err on the side of putting other kids down, and his football coach has said a few things here and there, but we think he's afraid to say too much, because he's worried Avery will quit and they need him. We've held off saying much because we don't want to make Avery feel bad, but things can't continue as they are. We didn't raise him to be arrogant, and this sounds awful, but sometimes when I hear him I'm so ashamed to be his parent.

If Peter and Lisa continue to ignore Avery's attitude, odds are it'll get worse. And as people start to tire of his overconfidence and speak their mind, his self-esteem will take a hit. Avery needs to be brought down a notch or two, so people calling him out on his arrogance isn't necessarily a bad thing. But if tensions have been building for a while, he'll be confronted with an avalanche of animosity, and that will do more harm than good. Helping him to see the need to change before it gets to this point is the kinder approach.

Peter and Lisa need to start calling Avery out on his cockiness. They'll need to choose their words wisely so as not to batter his self-esteem in the process, but helping Avery notice the impact of his attitude is a necessary step. Comments like 'Why are you always so cocky? Nobody likes it. You're not nearly as good as you think you are' aren't going to be helpful. Neutral, de-personalised comments are what's needed (e.g. 'I think when you said that, you gave other people the impression that you think they're dumb and you're better than them. I think you really hurt Sam's feelings.'). If Avery really has no idea what arrogant behaviour is, Peter and Lisa will also need to go through specific examples with him, and help him to explore the pros and cons of arrogance so he has a better understanding of the potential consequences of his current behaviour.

Once Avery more clearly understands the downsides of arrogance, Peter and Lisa can help him set specific modesty goals that encourage a more humble and supportive attitude, for example, 'I will resist the urge to take credit for wins on the football field and will make sure I compliment my teammates when they play well' or 'I won't brag about my school marks, and if someone asks, I'll say I did okay and then change the subject. If someone seems upset about their mark, I can offer to help them study for the next test.' Because habits can be hard to break, Peter and Lisa will need to keep a close eye on Avery's behaviour over the coming weeks. When Avery demonstrates modest, supportive behaviour, they'll need to praise him for this and reward him for his efforts, at least in the short-term while he learns to let go of his arrogant mindset. If Avery doesn't make any progress with rewards, or if there are instances where his arrogance is hurtful to others, consequences should be brought into play. Withdrawing privileges will work well, though logical consequences (being sent off for part of the game or having to miss the first fifteen minutes of practice) will probably be more powerful.

Whatever the cause, like low confidence, overconfidence can be fixed. Correctly identifying the underlying cause of your child's overconfidence is essential, though, because a mismatch between cause and strategy can make things worse. Thinking that learnt overconfidence is actually a front for low confidence, for example, is problematic, because the confidence-building strategies you need to correct low confidence can actually make learnt overconfidence worse. If what you're doing doesn't seem to be working, or if things seem to be getting worse, a mismatched approach might be the issue. Don't give up. Rethink your initial hypothesis and change your approach accordingly.

The important bits

+ Once your child's old enough to gauge their level of competence relative to same-aged peers, building confidence requires a holistic approach.

+ If you try to build confidence by protecting your child from failure and disappointment, you could end up making things worse.

+ Confidence isn't a quick fix. A longer-term approach is key.

+ Help your child develop a balanced approach to achievement by finding activities they can excel in, celebrating courage over and above outcome-based achievements, and encouraging personal bests.

+ Help your child to feel important by listening actively (not half-heartedly), setting aside quality time on a regular basis, and supporting their friendships.

+ Help your child develop a confident attitude by encouraging kind self-talk and helping them to view their mistakes as an opportunity to learn.

+ Help your child feel capable by tasking them with their own set of responsibilities, helping them to learn how to solve problems on their own, giving them the opportunity to do things for themselves, and letting them make their own decisions.

+ Don't be overly complimentary and tell your child they're good at things if they're not.

+ Don't set expectations that are impossible for your child to meet.

+ Your words matter, so don't speak to your child in a way that will damage their self-esteem.

+ Overconfidence can be just as problematic as low confidence. If overconfidence is an issue for your child, determine the cause, then work to help them be more modest and supportive of others.

5.

WHEN YOUR CHILD IS FACED WITH DIVORCE

No one goes into marriage thinking it'll end in divorce, yet for about half of all marriages, that's exactly what happens, and it's horrendous. There's the initial shock and grief over the end of your marriage, feelings of failure (for the record, you haven't failed; you've identified there's nothing more you can do to make your relationship work), fear of what's to come, and if divorce isn't something you want, anger at your partner's willingness to throw everything away.

If you have a child, divorce is even more complicated. Even though your marriage has reached its expiration date, your co-parenting relationship hasn't. Like it or not, your child means you're tied to your ex always and forever — a depressing thought, I know. But there are two ways you can play this: continue to hate on your ex and have conflict bind you together for life; or put aside your personal feelings about your ex and commit to being the best co-parent you can for the sake of your child. Making your co-parenting relationship your priority will work a whole lot better for you longer term as well.

There's a lot that'll change for your child with divorce. He or she will have to adjust to living across two homes and not seeing Mum and Dad on a daily basis; there'll be changes to everyday routines, greater financial restrictions (which might mean fewer after school or weekend activities); and potentially a change of school and loss of the family home as well. What your child doesn't need on top of everything else is two parents who openly hate each other, like Louise and Paul.

Louise

" When we separated we said we'd keep things friendly for the kids' sake, but we can't even be in the same room. He doesn't care about us at all. He says he wants a 50/50 parenting agreement which is ridiculous because he travels all the time with work. He's just trying to hurt me.

I'm really trying to give the kids stability because I know that's important, but Paul's trying to sell the house from underneath us. It's so wrong. He's already moved on with someone else. All he cares about is having enough money to start a new family with her. I've told the kids not to worry, that there's no way I'm going to let him take the house, but they're still upset.

Paul

❝ Louise didn't want a divorce so she's punishing me by turning the kids against me. She's convinced I had an affair and that's why I left — it's not. I am seeing someone, but that's only new. I've tried to set the record straight, but she isn't interested.

Louise wants to keep the family home, which is fine, but if she keeps the house, her child support will be less, and she won't accept that. She's told the kids I'm trying to force her to sell, which isn't true, and now they're really angry. I tried to tell them my side of the story but they're too angry.

Louise is in the kids' ears telling them what I bad parent I am. I'll admit, I'm busy at work so there are times I have to cancel plans last minute, but I can't help that.

Louise is acting like I've abandoned the kids, which I never would. I'm divorcing her, not our kids. She needs to stop before she ruins my relationship with them completely.

Louise and Paul might each think they're the wronged party, but despite their differences, they have one important thing in common: they both love their kids. Only problem is, they're both too busy playing the blame game to see that where their kids are concerned, they're actually both in the wrong. Louise is so consumed by anger and hurt, she hasn't realized that by bringing the kids into adult issues (like the details of the financial settlement) she's adding to their distress and inadvertently sabotaging the very thing she knows is important: stability. Likewise, Paul is so intent on blaming Louise for the quality of his relationship with his kids that he's not yet considered that his own actions might be part of the problem. If he wants a strong relationship with his kids — and a more amicable relationship with Louise — he needs to make his kids a priority, and that means showing up when he's said he will.

Your divorce will affect your child. With so much change, it can't not, but how your child copes will ultimately come down to one thing: how well they're protected from adult conflict. Kids whose parents shield them from adult issues through divorce fare far better than kids whose parents feel the need to vent about their co-parent's wrongdoings and character flaws. In fact, studies show that when kids with divorced parents are protected from adult arguments, they perform as well on measures of wellbeing as children of low-conflict continuously married parents. This is an important finding in and of itself, but even more significant when you consider the huge body of research showing that children of divorced parents usually have lower self-esteem and more emotional, behavioural and social issues than children of non-divorced parents.

The good news is, you can control how much exposure your child has to adult conflict, at least at your end. The bad news is, you're divorcing (or have already divorced) your ex for good reason, and conflict will probably be a regular part of your co-parenting relationship, at least in the early years. But you can dislike your co-parent and disagree with their parenting decisions and still co-parent effectively and protect your child from adult friction. Will be it easy? Nope. But it *will* get easier. Having the right strategies in place will speed things up, which is why you need to keep reading.

Breaking the divorce news

Once you know you're getting a divorce, your first task is telling your child, and there's no easy way to do this. No matter which way you spin it, your child's going to be upset, and that's okay. There are a few things you can do to make it easier for your child to digest. If you can, plan what you'll say with your co-parent ahead of time, and break the divorce news together. 'We both love you and we'll always be here for you' will carry a lot more weight if you're both present. If there's too much conflict at play for a joint approach to work, agree on a narrative and deliver the news in separate conversations, ideally within a reasonably short window of time. Exactly what you say will depend on your child and their needs, but something like the below is a good starting point.

> We want to talk to you about some changes that will be happening in our family. Mum/Dad and I have been having a lot of trouble getting along. It has nothing to do with you. None of our fights are your fault, it's us. We haven't been getting along for quite a long time. We've tried really hard to fix things, but we haven't been able to, so we've decided that the best way for our family to be happy is for Mum/Dad and I to live separately. Living separately means we'll be getting a divorce.
>
> Even though there will be things that will change, lots of things will stay the same. We both love you and that will never change. You'll still see both of us each week and you can call either of us whenever you want. You'll still go to the same school and do all the same activities, and you can still see your friends on weekends.

What will be different is that on some nights you'll stay at Mum's house with her and Dad will stay at his house, and on other nights you'll stay at Dad's house with him, and Mum will stay at her house.

It will be sad to not all live together anymore, and it will take some getting used to, but we've given this a lot of thought and we think this is the right thing for our family. If you have any questions about divorce and how things will work, you can ask us anything you like. There are some things we're still working out, so we may not always have all the answers you need straight away, but we'll do our best to answer any and all of your questions, and if there's one we can't answer, we'll come back to you as soon as we can. And if you feel sad or worried or mad, we get it. You can always talk to us and tell us how you feel. We love you and we're always here for you, no matter where we live.

You'll notice that in the above, the exact reason for the divorce is vague and non-specific, and that's exactly how it should be. It doesn't matter how old your child is, they don't need to know that Mum/Dad has been having an affair or that Mum/Dad is lazy and unsupportive. These are adult issues, and no matter how admissible they seem to you, when it comes to your child's parent relationships, they're irrelevant. You can tell yourself that your child deserves to know the truth, but, whether you're willing to admit it or not, in reality, you really only want to lay bare your co-parent's dirty laundry so your child sides with you and sees their Mum/Dad in the same light you do. Bringing your child into adult issues will only add to their confusion and distress, so do the right thing and take the high road instead. It's the harder path to take, but there'll come a day when your child thanks you for it.

No matter how you decide to tell your child, what you want to make clear is that even though some things will change, lots of things will stay the same, including how much your child is loved by Mum and Dad. Your child may find it hard to take everything in, especially if they're really upset, so be prepared to have the same conversation a few times over before your child really comprehends the magnitude of what you're saying. Make sure they know they can come to you with questions, and show them you mean this by checking in with them regularly to see if there's anything they want to talk about. And as hard as this will be, try to stay as unemotional as possible when talking to your child about your divorce. If you're noticeably upset (and keep in mind your child will be on high alert to see if you are) it'll be hard for your child to have confidence in you when you tell them everything will be okay. Your child will follow your lead. If you're okay, they'll be okay. If you're feeling too raw, take the time you need to process things yourself before breaking the news to your child. Your child needs to hear the news sooner rather than later, and it's important they hear it from you, but a few days won't matter.

Developing a parenting plan

Your parenting plan will dictate when your child sees each parent, how parenting decisions (big or small) will be made, and how you'll communicate with your co-parent about any issues or concerns if and when they arise. There are three ways you can do this. If you have a decent relationship with your co-parent and can set aside your personal feelings to prioritize your child's needs, coming to an agreement over coffee might be a possibility. If things are a little tense and you and your co-parent have different ideas about what's in your child's best interest, mediation might be better. And if things are pretty hostile, too much even for mediation, court might end up being your only way forward. If that's the case, remember your child's needs must still come first. When you hire a lawyer, you're the client. Not your child; you. And your lawyer will fight to get you what you want, no matter how much conflict this causes, no matter what's actually in your child's best interest, and no matter how much it costs. Don't fall into that trap. You're going to have to co-parent with your ex for the rest of your life. How you act now will set the tone for this relationship. Get draw into a battle over who's made the most parenting mistakes and who's the worse parent and your relationship may never recover, which will have damaging effects for your child. As much as it'll kill you, take the high road. Put your child's needs above your own overwhelming desire to throw the book at your ex, and if your ex doesn't play by the same rules, well, two wrongs don't make a right. If at least one parent is putting your child's needs first, they'll be far better off.

When you're developing your parenting plan, there's really only one rule: make decisions with your child's best interest at heart. Don't make decisions based on anger, don't prioritize your own needs and happiness, and don't put your child in the uncomfortable position of having to make adult decisions. Regardless of what's transpired between you and your ex, no matter how abhorrent you find them, and no matter how angry you are at past betrayals, your child needs you to put them first. Being a good co-parent is probably one of the hardest things you're ever going to have to do, even more so if your relationship hasn't ended amicably, but your child needs you to protect them. And if your co-parent really is as bad as you think they are, there's even more reason for you to step up and be the adult your child needs you to be. How much your child is affected by the breakdown of your marriage depends on what you do next; keep that front of mind as you negotiate.

Parent contact

When it comes to parent contact hours, you might wish your co-parent would fall off the face of the Earth, but unless you have serious concerns about abuse or neglect, regular and frequent time with both parents is in your child's best interests. This will differ depending on your family and the age of your child, but as a general rule, your child will benefit from relatively frequent, consistent and predictable time with both parents, without too many handovers. Parenting plans that involve multiple handovers through the week are confusing, and as your child gets older, a big inconvenience for all involved. Plans that involve long blocks of time without contact with one parent are equally problematic, though, especially for younger children, so they should be avoided where possible as well. If week-about access isn't possible (either because of your child's age or due to one parent's work schedule) then plans that include weekend access with at least one afternoon/evening are usually ideal.

If your child's around ten years or older they're likely to appreciate the opportunity to put forward their opinions and preferences for contact. Listening to their thoughts is a good thing — feeling heard helps kids adjust — but no child should be put in the awkward position of having to say who they want to live with, no matter what their age. Think about how you'd feel if someone forced you to choose between your children — not so great. By all means, ask your child whether there's anything they'd like the adults to take into consideration, but make it clear that it's the adults who will ultimately make decisions about living arrangements.

Handovers done right

For a multitude of reasons, handovers are rarely done well. Whether it's passive aggressive digs, high levels of adult distress or an overall iciness, your child will be far more aware of the dynamics between you and your co-parent than you realize, so you need to be on your best behaviour, no matter how difficult that is. You have every right to feel emotional at handovers. They can be rough, especially when a separation is relatively new. But they're also hard for your child, which is why you can't let them see your distress. Seeing you distressed will make your child feel insecure and upset, and it will affect their time with their other parent. They'll worry about you and feel responsible for your wellbeing, and that's a burden too great for little shoulders.

For your child's sake, handovers need to be neutral and friendly, even positive. Even if it kills you, the best thing you can do for your child is to be pleasant and cheerful, and that includes saying hello to your co-parent and briefly making small talk. Phrases like 'I'm going to miss you so much!' should be avoided. Language like this has the potential to make your child feel guilty about leaving you; so instead, use more positively geared phrases like 'Have a great time with Mum/Dad and I'll see you at the weekend!' If your child starts to show signs of distress, a long drawn out goodbye won't help. Your parenting instincts will compel you to stay, but staying will only make things worse, especially if you start to get upset as well. Say goodbye, walk away, and know that your child will be okay. If an update from your co-parent after the fact will make this easier, set this up ahead of time away from little ears.

If handovers continue to be emotionally traumatic for either you or your child, organize school-day handovers. One parent can do drop-off and the other pick-up, and any belongings can be left at the school office or dropped at your co-parent's house while your child is at school. If your child's yet to start school, use a similar approach with any recurring activities your child participates in, or try doing handovers in a public, neutral environment to lessen their intensity. Keeping things calm at handover will go a long way towards helping your child to cope, so do whatever you can do to keep things harmonious.

Keep things the same where you can

A lot will change for your child post-divorce, most of it unavoidable, so keeping what you can consistent is key. Keep up your child's usual routines — morning routines, after-school activities, evening and bedtime routines — across both households, and try to stick to your normal household rules and behavioural standards as well — again, across both households if at all possible. Special treats (skipping after-school activities to have a milkshake, getting a free pass from homework, staying up late) or a more relaxed approach to rules and boundaries might seem like a good idea, especially if you're worried about how well your child's coping with your divorce, but changing the rules when so much has changed already can backfire. Consistent routines and boundaries make your child's environment predictable, and this predictability is what that will help your child to feel safe, secure and reassured. Abandoning your usual rules and consequences might help alleviate your child's distress in the short term, but longer term it can cause feelings of anxiety, unsettledness and confusion.

Your child needs you to keep what you can in their life the same, and that means parenting them the way you always have, divorce or no divorce. What you can change is the way you go about enforcing boundaries — you can enforce them with more compassion. Consider this scenario. You've asked your child three times to get dressed for school. Not only is he not dressed yet, you've just caught him playing games on your iPad which he knows he's not allowed to do. When you asked him to hand over the iPad, he made a huge song and dance about it and refused to give it to you. You're furious, but it's your child's first week back at school since the separation so you don't know what to do. You don't want to let things go completely because his behaviour has been atrocious, but you also don't want to lose it at him because you know he's upset about the divorce and is usually a pretty good kid. That's where compassionate boundaries come in.

Setting compassionate boundaries means you uphold your usual boundaries while also acknowledging and showing compassion for your child's distress. This meets your child's need for consistency and their need for emotional validation. It might look something like this.

" Parent: *(after taking a few minutes to cool off and in a calm, empathic voice)* I want to talk to you about what just happened. I know you know you're meant to be getting ready for school, and you also know you're not supposed to use my iPad without asking, or yell at me like that. You usually get ready for school really well and we don't usually fight like this, so I'm wondering if maybe you're feeling a bit sad about the separation and it's making you feel funny about going to school today?

Child: I miss Mum/Dad. I don't want to move and I don't want to not all live together. And I don't know what I'm supposed to say to my friends.

Parent: *(choosing to prioritize emotional support over reprimands for poor behaviour)* I know it's really hard and I know you miss Mum/Dad. Things are going to feel a bit different for a while, but it'll get better. Mum/Dad and I both love you and we're sorry this is so hard. We're both here for you and you can always talk to us. Would it help if I talked to your teacher so someone at school knows what's happening at home?

Child: *(nods)*

Parent: And I could talk to your friends' parents as well if you'd like, so you don't have to worry about people not knowing yet. And either they can tell your friends, or you can tell your friends that your mum and dad are getting a divorce and they're going to be living in different houses. If friends ask you questions you don't know the answers to, it's okay to say, 'I'm not sure', and if it's something you're worried about, you can come home and ask me or Mum/Dad about it and we can answer any questions you have, does that sound like a good plan?

Child: *(seeming a bit happier)* Yep.

Parent: *(knowing a boundary still needs to be set, and in a warm, understanding voice)* Good. Mum/Dad and I are here to help you and you can always come to us. It's okay to feel upset, and it's okay to feel frustrated, you have every right to feel like that right now, but it's not okay to not listen and not stick to the house rules, and it's not okay to yell at me like that. If you're feeling upset or worried you can tell me and we'll figure it out together, but you need to use your words and not misbehave.

Child: *(seeming a bit sheepish)* I know.

Parent: I'm not going to take screen time away all together, but I am going to say that because of your behaviour this morning, you can't use my iPad for the next two days. We can still watch a movie together tonight on TV, but you can't use my iPad for games. And next time, we'll both try to handle things differently.

Child: Okay.

Real-world conversations obviously never run as perfectly as scripted conversations like this, but you get the general idea. You can meet your child's emotional needs and uphold your usual boundaries by slightly changing your approach. Your child will feel heard and understood and know you're willing to help, but they'll also understand that divorce or no divorce, your expectations haven't changed: you still expect compliance and the respectful behaviour you know your child's capable of. And if you're ever unsure where to draw the line, ask yourself how you would have handled misbehaviour prior to your divorce and do that — but with compassion.

Be flexible with contact hours

If your child wants to see or speak to your co-parent during their time with you, let them. Not reluctantly or with an air of passive aggression, but in a way that lets your child know you completely support them having contact with their other parent. Yes, it's your scheduled time, but you don't own your child and your child has the right to feel connected to you and your co-parent at all times no matter what your schedule says. Most times, knowing you're willing to be flexible will help your child feel more comfortable, often to the extent that their need for contact with their other parent is less, but if their requests for time with their other parent increase or are so frequent that they're starting to interfere with how well they settle with you, take a step back and look at what needs to be different.

By seeking out frequent contact with your co-parent, your child's letting you know that they're not coping. They might be feeling conflicted about being away from your co-parent, either due to guilt or worry; or if your co-parent is in the family home, their desire to see them might be more about that than anything else. Talk to your child and try to understand how they're feeling and why. No matter what your child says, don't get mad or minimize their feelings, just listen and let them know that you understand and you're sorry they're having such a tough time.

Once you've got a better idea of what's underlying their need for such regular contact with your co-parent, look at possible solutions. If your child misses their usual bedroom, look at what you can do to make their new bedroom in your home feel more comfortable and familiar. If your child misses your co-parent when they're with you, tell them that that's okay, you completely understand, and see if having more regular phone contact with Mum/Dad would help. And if your child's having trouble settling because they're worried about your co-parent, speak to your co-parent about this, but think through your approach first. Accusing your co-parent of sabotaging your time with your child or blaming them for your child's distress will get you nowhere fast. Don't dictate instructions or put demands on your co-parent, ask for their help. Let them know that your child is having a hard time settling when they're with you, in part because they're worried your co-parent is sad and lonely when they're not there to keep them company. Make it clear that you're not accusing your co-parent of putting this idea in their head (even if you suspect that's the case), that you think it's just part and parcel of your child adjusting to the divorce. Then ask whether your co-parent can help by talking to your child about things they've done or people they've seen, so your child knows they're out and about and not suffering in silence at home.

Once you've asked, leave it at that. The more insistent you are, the more resistant your co-parent will be to actioning your suggestion. If things are really strained, ask your co-parent for their ideas on what might help your child to feel more comfortable when they're with you;

a two-sided approach like this will help to defuse any defensiveness on your co-parent's part and increase the likelihood of them listening to your original suggestion. And be open to taking these ideas on board. It's hard to ask for help and communicate from a vulnerable position, especially if you and your co-parent don't get along, but it'll help you to be more effective in the long run, and that'll make it worth it.

If your child doesn't want to spend time with you

If your co-parent gives you feedback that your child doesn't want to spend time in your home, one of two things is probably happening. Either your child's having a hard time separating from your co-parent, or you're doing something that's making your child uncomfortable.

In either case, if you're given feedback like this, listen. Don't assume your co-parent's making things up or coercing your child into saying things they don't mean, and don't assume the issue is at your co-parent's end and has nothing to do with you. Don't put your child on the spot and pump them for information on whether they like spending time with you. Not only will your questions make your child uncomfortable (which, if the issue lies with you, will only make things worse) they won't get you very far. It takes a healthy dose of confidence and some pretty well-developed assertiveness skills to answer a question like this honestly, and your child has neither yet. So, when your child tells you they love spending time with you, it won't really be all that telling, because chances are they'll respond this way even if they don't enjoy being around you, not because they're free of your co-parent's influence, but because they don't feel comfortable telling you the truth.

If you're told your child isn't enjoying their time with you, think on why that might be. Perhaps you're not making enough time for your child on the weeks they stay with you? Do you make comments about your co-parent in front of, or near, your child that make your child uncomfortable? Does your child have their own space in your home yet? When it comes to activities, do you sometimes say no to things your child wants to do because they fall on 'your' weeks and you don't want to lose precious time, even if it means your child misses out?

Your child's reluctance to spend time with you could come down to any number of things, but the above reasons tend to be the most common. Note that they all relate to your child's needs and your relationship with your child; they have nothing to do with your co-parent. Ask your co-parent for help in better understanding why your child's reluctant to spend time with you if you're really struggling to make sense of it, but don't assume they're at fault. Issues around separation and your co-parent's behaviour at handovers might be playing a role as well, but don't get so distracted by this that you forget to look at what *you're* doing that might be contributing to the issue. Fix what's happening at your end first, and if time with you remains an issue, then look at how you can raise your other concerns with your co-parent effectively.

If your child doesn't like going to Mum/Dad's house

Kids often feel the need to protect their parents' feelings after a divorce, so if your child tells you they don't like going to your co-parent's house, listen, but don't react too strongly. Unless you have concerns about abuse or neglect, the worst thing you can do is overreact and stop supporting your co-parent's time with your child. For starters, there's a good chance your child's telling you what they think you want to hear. Even if that's not the case and your child genuinely dislikes spending time with your co-parent, their reasons might not be entirely valid. Your co-parent might insist that your child finish all their vegetables before they leave the table, for example, or they might not allow screen time after dinner, which aren't all together unreasonable requests, even if they aren't rules you follow in your household.

See if you can help your child come up with a plan for improving their time with your co-parent. Start by letting your child know you want them to feel happy and comfortable in both homes, and ask for their ideas on what might help with this. Give them time to come up with their own ideas, but if they're having trouble, things like having more special one-on-one time with their other parent, being able to take more of their belongings between houses, or talking to their other parent about their concerns usually help. Not only will this process lead to actionable solutions, but it also shows your child that you want them to enjoy their time with your co-parent, which, if tiptoeing around your feelings has been part of the issue, will help to make things better from this end as well.

Give your co-parent a heads-up that this is a conversation you've had, but be sensitive in your approach. If you bluntly tell them that your child's told you they don't want to spend time with them, they won't react well and, to be fair, neither would you if the situation was reversed. Let your co-parent know that your child has alluded to the fact that they're unhappy moving between houses, so you've spoken with them about what they can do to fix this. Stress that you've really tried to reinforce to your child that you want them to be happy at both houses in case that's the reason for their disclosure, and let your co-parent know you're happy to talk things through further if they'd like. This might go against your initial instincts, but that doesn't mean it's not the right approach. Give it a try, and if things don't improve, or if your child shows signs of distress after spending time with your co-parent, take further action and seek professional advice; but before you do, make sure further action is actually warranted and not a knee-jerk reaction on your part to adult conflict. Remember, your goal is to protect your child from conflict. Reflect on that before you take any unnecessary action.

Respect your child's time with their co-parent

When your child is with your co-parent, try to be respectful of their time. Your child has a right to uninterrupted time with their other parent and their needs trump yours. If your child initiates contact with you, by all means make time to take their call and hear about their happenings, but try not to contact them over and above what's been discussed, no matter how much you miss them. Don't repeatedly call your child and get upset when they can't talk, and don't force your child to speak to you just because it's your allocated call time. You might be ready to chat at your scheduled time, but that doesn't mean your child will be. Planned phone calls are there for your child's benefit, not yours. Insisting that your child talk to you regardless of whether they're in the mood to chat will not only put your child in a worse mood, but it also won't do your relationship any favours. Know that your child loves you and try not to take their indifference personally. Your child's just in a mood. The good news is it'll pass, and if you don't make an issue of it, the next phone call will be different.

No matter how desperately you miss your child, and how much you dislike your co-parent, don't buy your child a phone and sneak it into their backpack so you can call them whenever you want to. Your intentions might be good, but operating behind your co-parent's back puts your child in a terrible position. They now have to keep your secret for the duration of their time with their other parent, with the added pressure of making sure they catch your calls so as not to upset you. Not having the freedom to be with your child whenever you like is probably the worst part of divorce and will take a while to adjust to. But, as hard as it is, your child's needs must come first. Find ways to look after yourself when your child's away from you, and give it time. It'll take a while, but it will get easier.

Avoid negative comments, but make nice as well

The unhelpfulness of making negative comments about your co-parent in front of your child is something you've probably already considered. What you might not have thought about is that because your child is incredibly perceptive with superhuman hearing to boot, you need to refrain from speaking negatively about your co-parent anytime your child is within a 200-metre (220 yard) radius. That means not making negative comments, whispered or otherwise, to others during phone calls when your child's in the next room, and not discussing adult issues any time your child's remotely nearby. Your child might appear to be preoccupied and unaware of your conversation, but odds are they're hearing more than you realize. Your child has a right to a healthy relationship with both parents. Hearing your negativity will confuse and upset your child. By all means vent, but do so in private and well out of earshot of your child.

For your child's sake, don't just avoid negativity: make the effort to make positive comments about your co-parent. When your child gives you a blow-by-blow description of all the fun things they did with Mum/ Dad over the weekend and you respond with a drawn out silence or a lukewarm 'That's nice', your message is clear: 'I don't want to hear this.' From an adult perspective, your unenthusiastic response is completely understandable. Hearing about the parts of your child's life that you're no longer part of is a painful reminder of all that you've lost and just how different things now are. But your child doesn't think like an adult. He or she is too young to understand the emotional complexities of your divorce, so when you react with indifference, your child draws their own conclusions instead, like, 'I've done something wrong' or 'I've upset Mum/Dad and she/he is mad at me'.

Your child needs to know it's okay for them to talk to you about their time with your co-parent. It'll take some getting used to, but when your child talks excitedly about what they did with Mum/Dad, ask questions to show you're interested, and make sure your child knows you've loved hearing all about their weekend. Make positive statements, even if it kills you, because that's what your child needs you to do (e.g. 'That's so great that Mum/Dad organized that for you, what a fun way to spend the weekend!'). It'll be hard at the start, but it will get easier, and your efforts will make the world of difference to your child.

Signs your child might not be coping

Even if you get everything right, your child might still have difficulty adjusting to your divorce. If your child's older, they might be able to put into words how they're feeling, but odds are they're more likely to communicate their distress behaviourally. Common signs of distress are things like:

- increased tearfulness
- changes to sleep and eating habits
- clinginess or distress at times of separation (including bedtime)
- uncharacteristic challenging behaviour or a worsening of usual problem behaviours
- nightmares

- regular stomach aches or headaches
- signs of sadness or anger
- withdrawing and seeming quieter than usual
- recurrence of past soothing behaviours (e.g. thumb-sucking).

Take action if your child starts to show signs of distress. Look at what you can change to better support their adjustment (e.g. more frequent contact with both parents or increased protection against parent conflict) and if things don't improve, seek additional help.

Collaborative co-parenting vs parallel parenting

Your parenting plan will also need to include guidelines for decision making and communication, so you'll need to decide whether you're going to adopt a collaborative co-parenting or parallel parenting approach. Collaborative co-parenting involves both parents remaining actively involved in their child's life and putting aside their individual differences to communicate respectfully and work effectively together as a parenting team. In a parallel parenting approach, both parents continue to play an active role in their child's life and share parenting responsibilities, but they do so in parallel, with as little direct contact as possible. Major parenting decisions (e.g. relating to health or education) are still made jointly, but day-to-day decisions — bedtime, screen time limits, weekend activities — are decided individually without co-parent consultation.

Generally speaking, collaborative co-parenting is the better approach. When done properly, a collaborative approach will protect your child from adult conflict, which will in turn help them to feel safe, secure and loved, even in the midst of divorce. But before you adopt this approach, you need to be honest with yourself about your ability to put aside your personal feelings about your ex to co-parent effectively with them. Think carefully about whether it's an approach that will work for your family before you make a commitment either way.

Collaborating with your co-parent on decisions

If you do decide to go with a collaborative approach, sit down with your co-parent to negotiate guidelines for decision making. The more specific you are, the more successful your parenting plan will be, so cover as many areas as you can. Be clear about your expectations for what will need to be decided jointly, such as living arrangements, which schools your child will attend, health care. And discuss your expectations for day-to-day decision making — things like after-school activity schedules, play dates and birthday parties.

For day-to day decisions, keep your co-parent in the loop regardless of whether an activity falls on your contact days. If it's an activity that falls on one of your co-parent's days, you definitely need to check with them first before giving your child a yes or no. Don't tell your child that you don't have a problem with them playing baseball this season or going to Hannah's birthday party at the weekend but you have to check with Mum/Dad to see if they agree; you'll inadvertently expose your child to adult conflict and subtly sabotage their relationship with your co-parent. Let your child know that you'll need to chat to Mum/Dad so you can decide together, but you'll come back to them as soon as you can with a final outcome. Talk to your co-parent in private, then give your child feedback, making sure that feedback is neutral. If you disagree with your co-parent's decision, it'll be hard to bite your tongue, but highlighting your co-parent's failings for your child helps no-one, and years from now when your child remembers the subtle ways you made digs at their Mum/Dad, they'll resent you for it.

If there's any residual anger on your part towards your co-parent, or if you're struggling to be away from your child when they spend time with their mum/dad, it'll be tempting to schedule activities so they coincide with your co-parent's time rather than your own. Don't. Passive aggressive actions like this won't help, they'll just lead to hurt and anger. Respect your child's time with their co-parent and try to keep your own feelings separate. And if you're reluctant to let your child attend birthday parties or other extracurricular activities because you don't want to miss out on time with them, think twice before you say no. You don't own your child and you're not entitled to them. Your child didn't ask for divorced parents and they shouldn't have to miss out on activities because of it. There will be times you need to say no for other reasons, but be honest about your motives and make sure you're not saying no because you're rigidly holding on to the hours and minutes you think you're entitled to. You might think you're doing it to protect your relationship with your child, but odds are if you're too rigid and inflexible, your child will end up resenting you for it. Think about what your child needs and be guided by that.

Communicating effectively with your co-parent

Your collaborative parenting plan will also need to cover ground rules for communication. Decide at the outset what warrants communication and what doesn't. Major decisions, like moving to a new house or introducing a new partner, should definitely be on the 'warrant communication' list. You might think what you do in your personal life isn't any of your ex's business, and as far as your personal relationship with your ex goes, you're right, but issues like this affect your child, so your co-parent needs to be kept in the loop. If you don't communicate about big issues like this, you put your child in the difficult position of feeling confused about whether they're supposed to keep your news a secret or, worse, having to break the news to your co-parent on your behalf. Neither scenario is fair or reasonable. You don't to have to share every little thing that happens in your life, but for your child's sake, you need to make open and honest communication with your co-parent a priority.

You'll also need to agree on what needs to be communicated day-to-day. Changes to plans for parent contact, scheduled appointments and homework are areas of communication that will come up a lot, and if your child's involved in lots of different activities, things will definitely fall through the cracks if you don't have a good day-to-day communication system in place. There are lots of great apps to help. Shared online calendars like Google Calendar are a great way to make sure everyone's across key activities and appointments, but there's also a great range of apps designed specifically for separated and divorced parents, like Our Family Wizard. There's a subscription fee attached to it, but features like the ability to track your parenting schedule, share appointment details, and submit requests for one-time changes to parenting time makes it worth it. You can also keep track of shared parenting expenses and receipts, make notes about any issues of concern, and share important information like school or homework schedules, medical histories and emergency contacts. Communicating via SMS or email is also an option, but when it comes to logistics, the sheer volume of information that needs to be communicated means miscommunications and mistakes are more likely. If SMS or email work for you, great, but if they don't, invest time in finding a solution that works from the outset.

Rules for respectful communication

Respectful communication is key to you protecting your child from adult conflict, so it's especially important when it comes to co-parenting. Agreeing on what you communicate about is only half the battle; *how* you communicate — the words you use, your tone — is where the real challenge lies.

Rule number one: never communicate when you're angry. You'll be more likely to jump to conclusions and interpret neutral comments in a hostile or aggressive way. And because your co-parent is vulnerable to these same communication mishaps, things can get messy quickly. If your co-parent sends you a text that makes you see red, sit tight and give yourself 24 hours to cool off before you respond. If you're on a call and things start to get heated, say something like, 'I think we're both getting frustrated and this conversation isn't getting us anywhere. I'm going to hang up now but I'll call you tomorrow and we'll talk more then.' Make sure you call back when you say you will, or you'll add fuel to the fire. Resist the urge to argue and make effective communication your focus instead.

When in doubt, approach conversations with your co-parent, written or otherwise, in the same way you would a difficult client or colleague. Keep things business-like and neutral, and if you're having trouble deciding whether your communication is appropriate or not, ask yourself if you'd feel comfortable with your child overhearing your conversation or reading your emails, not because you'd allow this but because it'll help you keep yourself in check. Try to respond to correspondence from your co-parent (missed calls and voicemails included) within a reasonable timeframe, usually 24 to 48 hours. If you can't respond within this timeframe because you're busy at work or unwell, be transparent about this and let them know you'll reply as soon as you can, within three to four days at the latest.

Planning difficult conversations ahead of time will also help you communicate more effectively. The words you use and how you say them can mean the difference between your co-parent taking on board what you say versus not, so plan your approach wisely. If you want your co-parent to hear you, avoid blaming statements. They'll all but guarantee a defensive and ineffective discussion.

You can still let your co-parent know when you're unhappy about something, but you'll need to reframe critical, blame-oriented statements into assertive statements. A blame-oriented statement might be: 'You always make plans without checking with me first and assume I'm going to pick up the slack. You're so inconsiderate.' An assertive reframe of this might look like: 'I find it really hard when you make plans without checking with me first. It makes me feel like I have to say yes, and that makes me resentful. I really don't want to feel that way. I want to feel good about helping, not annoyed. I'd really like it if you can check my availability with me and not just assume I'm free.' Phrasing things this way helps your co-parent understand why you're upset, and because you've been clear about what you'd like to be different, they also know what they need to do to fix things. And because you've used neutral statements like 'when you make plans without checking with me first … it makes me feel resentful' your co-parent is more likely to hear what you have to say. Thinking ahead to how you can best approach conversations with your co-parent will be tiresome at first, but ongoing conflict is pretty energy zapping as well.

Giving your co-parent the information they need to understand your requests is another good strategy. When you need a favour, don't leave them guessing with statements like, 'I can't make school pick-up Thursday, I need you to get Ashleigh.' When emotions are involved, subtleties matter, and overly direct communications like this will seem disrespectful and rude. Instead, explain why you need help and acknowledge that your co-parent is doing you a favour by offering to help with something in return: 'I know it's short notice but I've had a meeting come up at work on Thursday, and it means I can't do school pick-up. Is there any chance you could help? I'd be happy to switch days in return if you'd like.' Same rules apply if you have to say no to a request. Don't just say, 'No can do.' Give context so your co-parent knows you're not saying no to be difficult, and try to offer an alternate solution if you can: 'I'm really sorry but I have a meeting that day too and can't get to school before 4.30 p.m. I can pick Ashleigh up from Lucy or Sam's house by 5 p.m. Do you want to see if either of their parents can do school pick-up? I can keep her from 5 p.m. until you can pick her up.' Going into so much detail will seem arduous, especially if your co-parent isn't coming to the party, but stick with it. You might not want to justify your requests or offer additional help, but if your goal is to protect your child from conflict, do it anyway. Let go of old hurts, hard as that may be, and communicate respectfully, and from a solution-focused standpoint, and things will run much more smoothly as a result.

You can keep communication respectful, too, by doing your research before you react. When your child inadvertently divulges information that makes you see red (e.g. 'Mum/Dad took me to meet a new friend of hers/his' or 'Mum/Dad left me home alone last week') hold back. First, whatever your concerns, they're adult issues and not issues your child needs to be brought into, which means not pumping your child for extra information and not giving away just how annoyed you really are. Second, you might not have all the facts. Your child might have forgotten to mention, for example that the 'friend' your co-parent introduced them to was their new boss or that they were 'left alone' for all of ten minutes while your co-parent walked the dog around the block. Before you make any knee jerk assumptions, ask your co-parent for clarification — respectfully: 'Max mentioned that you introduced him to a new friend on the weekend. I felt upset that you'd introduced him to someone you're seeing without talking to me first, but then I realized I was jumping to conclusions so wanted to ask you about it.' Try to give your co-parent the benefit of the doubt. It's easy to fall into the trap of assuming the worst of your co-parent, especially if they've given you cause in the past, but jumping to worst-case scenarios won't help, and neither will making mountains out of molehills. For your child's sake, and the sake of your co-parenting relationship, make 'ask before you assume' your new mantra.

When it comes to decision making and communication, don't assume you and your co-parent are on the same page; guarantee it with a clear, specific parenting plan. If conflict plays a significant role in your co-parenting relationship, a detailed plan is especially key. Negotiations will be rough going at times, but don't let anger and resentment guide your reactions. You'll be in a co-parenting relationship with your ex for the rest of your life; keeping things amicable is in everyone's best interest. And if your relationship with your co-parent is already amicable, don't get complacent. A detailed plan is by far the best way to keep things that way.

When respectful communication is anything but

If respectful communication is an issue even when it comes to relatively minor day-to-day issues, take action early on. Get a third party involved to help negotiate the terms of your parenting plan; this can be a mediator, a clinical psychologist with experience working with high-conflict divorced families, or a lawyer. And seriously consider whether a collaborative parenting plan is going to work, or whether you need to adopt a parallel approach instead. Remember, limiting your child's exposure to adult conflict is key, and in some families a parallel parenting plan is the best way to achieve this.

Parallel parenting isn't without its disadvantages. It means your child will need to adjust to two sets of house rules, and you'll have to adjust to two sets of rules as well, one of which you'll have no control over.

You might have strict rules in your home when it comes to sugar and screen time, but when your child's with their mum/dad, it's their house, their rules; you don't get a say. You can let your co-parent know that your child has netball Saturday and a birthday party on Sunday, but if it's your co-parent's weekend, whether your child goes to these events is completely at their discretion. And if your co-parent hires a nanny instead of asking for your help with school pick-ups, same rules apply. Not having control can be a hard pill to swallow, especially when your co-parent parents differently to you, but what will impact your child more: a missed birthday party and a few extra hours of screen time, or ongoing parent conflict?

Is it hard to relinquish control when your co-parent parents in a way you disagree with? Absolutely. Should you try to get your co-parent to see things from your point of view so they parent how you want them to? No. Your co-parent will resent your unsolicited advice, and may even deliberately do the opposite of what you've asked just to prove a point. The best thing you can do is stop focusing on the things you can't control, and make the things you can control — providing a happy, safe and loving environment within your home — your focus instead. Trust that your co-parent has your child's best interest at heart just as much as you do, even if their parenting looks different to yours, and know that, small stuff aside, what's really important is that your child feels loved by both parents and is protected from adult conflict. As hostilities and resentments fade with time, a more collaborative approach might be possible, but if that proves not to be the case, a parallel approach is the best way for you to meet your child's needs.

When you need help to keep things neutral

A parallel approach doesn't negate the need for communication, it just significantly lessens it. So if ongoing communication is an issue even with a parallel parenting arrangement and involving a third party on an ongoing basis isn't financially feasible, consider using a communication app. Our Family Wizard, which I mentioned on p. 171, has a messaging system that allows you to keep track of your correspondence with your co-parent. You can give a third party access to this correspondence if you wish, an option which can help all involved to be more mindful of considered and respectful communication. Even if you don't, once messages are sent, they can't be deleted or edited, and that in itself is usually enough to lessen hostile or aggressive correspondence.

Divvito is another great communication app. 'Dani' your personal messaging assistant scans your messages before sending them and suggests revisions where needed to keep communication neutral. The app also allows you to customize your communication preferences so you only receive messages from your co-parent at set times in the day: you can set up 'do not disturb' preferences, for example, so that you don't receive messages from your co-parent during business hours. It also helps organize messages into conversations so you can keep track of multiple discussions at the same time (e.g. changes to parenting arrangements, school holiday plans, shared expenses) so important information doesn't get lost or forgotten, minimizing the likelihood of unnecessary conflict.

Using an app to monitor your communications might seem extreme, but if conflict features heavily in your interactions, it might be your best bet.

Introducing new relationships

At one point or another, you and your co-parent may develop new relationships with significant others, and these people will become part of your child's life. How you handle this introduction is important. It doesn't matter how terrific your new partner is, seeing you with someone new will be a big adjustment for your child, and if your new partner has children, that adjustment will be bigger again. That you have a new partner will also solidify for your child that your divorce is permanent. You might have thought this is pretty obvious, especially if you've been separated for quite some time, but your child might have held out hope, and a new partner crushes this dream.

A new partner can also cause your co-parent distress, which, in turn, depending on how well that distress is hidden, can cause distress for your child. If your co-parent didn't want to separate, seeing you with someone new will no doubt trigger mixed feelings. Even if that's not the case, that a new person — and a possible new parent figure — is about to become a part of your child's life is confronting for most co-parents.

Introducing your child to your new partner is a big deal so don't gloss over it and pretend it's not. There's a right and a wrong way to go about things, so put some thought into your approach. First off, I can't stress enough how unhelpful it is to introduce your child to your new partner in the months after your divorce. Your child is still reeling and needs time to adjust. If you forge ahead with plans to play happy family too soon, it won't end well. Give your child time to adjust to the divorce, potentially twelve months. You'll encounter a few teething issues no matter when you take the leap, but less so if you wait.

When the time is right, talk to your co-parent first before making any introductions. It'll be an awkward conversation, but imagine if your co-parent introduced your child to their new partner without talking to you first. Not giving your co-parent a heads-up also puts your child in a hugely uncomfortable position. They'll feel pressure to keep your secret, whether you ask them to or not (and for the record, if you're considering asking your child to keep your new relationship a secret, don't; there's no scenario where this is a good idea). You'll also put them in the position of having to break your news to your co-parent, which, given it's a conversation you want to avoid yourself, is more than a little unfair. When the time comes, let your co-parent know that you're in a serious relationship and you'd like your new partner and your child to meet. So that your co-parent doesn't feel ambushed, let them know you'd like to do the introduction sometime in the next few weeks, but wanted to speak to them first to figure out the best approach, and give your co-parent the opportunity to have a coffee with your new partner first — with or without you present, whichever they'd prefer — if that's something they'd find helpful.

As a general rule, first meetings between your new partner and your child usually work best if they're time-limited, on neutral territory and planned well in advance. Meeting your new partner will be a lot for your child to process, so try not to overwhelm them with a long-winded first visit. Having your new partner sleep over definitely shouldn't be on the cards. Don't ask too many questions post-visit: What did you think? Did you like him/her? Do you want to spend more time with him/her? Is it okay with you if he/she comes over again next weekend? And don't throw your child in the deep end with a spontaneous meeting.

Give them plenty of notice that there's someone important you'd like them to meet, and make it clear that Mum/Dad has met this person and knows they'll be meeting them too. Let them know that you understand it might feel funny meeting your new partner, so they should let you know if there's anything you can do to make it easier, like your child picking the activity you all do together, giving your child the option to choose a time limit, or having a special code word your child can use if they feel uncomfortable. The more effort you put into preparing your child for your new relationship, the easier their adjustment will be, which means you'll be making your own life easier longer term as well. Try to be mindful of your child's feelings and let their best interests guide your approach.

And for subsequent meetings, take things slowly. Gradually increase the amount of time your child and your new partner spend together and, if you can, wait until your child's comfortable before you start overnight visits. If you end up moving in with your new partner, give your child plenty of advanced warning, and make special one-on-one time with them an ongoing priority. Remember, your child has had a lot to adjust to since your divorce, and stability is key. Having time with you is one of the constants they need to cope; make it something they can rely on.

Responding to your co-parent's new relationships

It's normal to feel ill at ease at a new partner coming into your child's life, no matter how solid your own relationship is, but this is an adult issue and one your child should be protected from. Your child loves you, so as soon as you make your feelings about Mum/Dad's new partner known, you put your child in an impossible position. If they let themselves like Mum/Dad's partner, they're betraying you; if they side with you and dislike them, they'll feel like they're doing the wrong thing by Mum/Dad. It's a lose–lose situation and one your child shouldn't be in.

Be positive about your co-parent's new partner, even if it kills you. When your child brings them up in conversation, don't stay quiet and hope that'll be enough. Make positive comments so your child knows they have your blessing (e.g. 'That sounds like a lot of fun and Paula/Paul sounds really nice. I'm really glad you had such a good weekend.'). If your child's reaction to your co-parent's new partner isn't positive, don't jump on the bandwagon. Validate their feelings, but don't reinforce their negative views. Say something like:

> 66 I'm sorry you didn't have a great weekend with Mum/Dad and things with Paula/Paul didn't get off to such a great start. You know what, I bet Paula/Paul was nervous meeting you because they know how special and important you are to Mum/Dad. Remember on your first day at school? You were worried you wouldn't make any friends. But now you've had time to get to know your classmates, you have lots of friends. Maybe this will be like that. How about you see Paula/Paul again before you make up your mind?

It's not your job to smooth the way for your co-parent and his/her new partner, but it is your job to protect your child from adult issues. Encouraging this new relationship will go against all your instincts, but it's the right thing to do, and one day your child will thank you for it.

The important bits

+ How well you protect your child from adult conflict will have a huge influence over how well they cope with your divorce.

+ Use language your child will understand to tell them about your divorce. Keep adult issues out of it, and help your child to understand what will be different and what will stay the same.

+ No matter what the circumstances, get a clear parenting plan in place from the outset. Set your own feelings aside and make decisions in your child's best interests.

+ Your child has a right to a happy, healthy relationship with both parents that's free of adult issues. Keep this in mind when you're making decisions about parent contact.

+ High conflict or high emotion handovers will be distressing for your child; keep things as neutral and pleasant as you can.

+ Your child needs stability, so keep things the same where you can, including your usual rules and boundaries.

+ Don't get so caught up in your hatred of your ex that you forget to listen to your child. If your child tells you they're not happy, listen.

+ Respect your child's time with their other parent. You might not like your ex, but your child has a right to a relationship with them that's free of your influence.

+ Your child has superhuman hearing; only vent about your ex when your child's nowhere remotely nearby.

+ If you can manage it, adopt a collaborative co-parenting approach. If conflict is an ongoing issue, consider a parallel parenting arrangement instead.

+ Set clear expectations for decision making and communication from the outset.
+ Make decisions that are in your child's best interests (not your own) and always, always communicate with your co-parent in a respectful way. If you can't, consider involving a third party or utilizing a communication app.
+ Introducing your child to a new partner is a big deal. Plan your approach carefully and involve your co-parent in the process.

6.

WHEN YOUR CHILD'S A WORRIER

When you're dealing with adult stressors like mortgage repayments, passive aggressive colleagues, and judgmental, intrusive in-laws, it's easy to write off worry about monsters under the bed, mistakes on homework and visits to the dentist as trivial. But kids can and do develop anxiety and they're doing so at an alarming rate.

In 2009, Professor Ronald Rapee and his colleagues conducted a research review and found that, worldwide, as many as 2.5 to 5 per cent of children and adolescents met criteria for an anxiety disorder.[1] Even more alarming, recent research indicates that prevalence rates now might be even higher. A report on the mental health of Australian children and adolescents released by the Australian government in 2015 showed that close to 7 per cent of all children aged between four and eleven met criteria for an anxiety disorder.[2] Just as concerning, a recent study published in the *Journal of Developmental and Behavioral Pediatrics* found that in the United States, rates of anxiety disorders amongst children aged between six and seventeen years increased from 4.7 per cent in 2007 to 5.3 per cent in 2011–12. That's a huge number of children affected by anxiety and a 13 per cent increase in childhood anxiety disorders in just four years.[3]

The good news is, there's a lot we can do to change that, but first things first: know what to look for.

What's normal and what's not?

Childhood anxiety disorders are a real and prevalent issue, but anxiety is also a normal emotion, and one all kids experience, even happy, healthy, confident kids. At the twelve- to eighteen-month mark, nearly all kids go through a phase of separation anxiety; a fear of animals, the dark, or loud noises is par for the course with most preschoolers; and it's not uncommon for school-aged children to worry about death, their school performance, germs and illness, natural disasters and other catastrophic events.[4] Normal developmental anxiety like this isn't cause for concern, but other types of anxiety might be, which is why knowing what to look for is key.

Normal developmental anxiety is reasonably harmless and relatively short-lived. But, anxiety attached to anxiety disorders causes considerable distress. It stops kids from participating in activities they'd like to be part of, and persists despite your efforts at reassurance and comfort. What's more, whereas symptoms of normal developmental anxiety are mostly emotional and behavioural, anxiety disorders often cause physical symptoms like headaches and stomach aches.

What are anxiety disorders?

The Diagnostic and Statistical Manual of Mental Health Disorders (DSM-5) lists seven main anxiety disorders; the four that affect kids most are outlined in the following table. If the symptoms seem familiar, keep in mind that to be considered a disorder, your child's symptoms need to be: persistent (lasting at least a month in the case of separation anxiety disorder, or six months in the case of generalized anxiety disorder, social anxiety disorder, or specific phobias), excessive (meaning they're more severe than would be considered normal for the situation), and severe enough to interfere with day-to-day functioning (including how your child functions at school, within the community and with peers).

If your child meets criteria for an anxiety disorder, intervene now. If they're showing signs and symptoms of anxiety on a regular basis, if they seem more anxious than other kids their age or more anxious than you think they should be given the situation, if anxiety stops them from enjoying activities or time with friends, or if it affects their ability to do things other kids their age can do, but they don't technically meet criteria for a full-blown disorder, chances are they'll still benefit from learning skills to cope with anxious symptoms, and the time to act is now. And if you're still not sure if your child's struggles are anxiety related, read on.

	Feature worry
Separation Anxiety Disorder	Fear that something bad will happen (either to a parent or themselves) when separation occurs, e.g. 'What if I get sick and my Mum/Dad isn't there to help me?'
Specific phobia (e.g. phobia about animals, needles, illness, costumed characters, spiders, loud noises, dark/night)	Worry that the feared object will cause harm.
Generalized Anxiety Disorder	Worry that something bad will happen across numerous domains. Worry might relate to sports performance, friendships, the health and safety of loved ones or child's own health, mistakes on schoolwork, academic performance, punctuality, etc, e.g. 'What if we're late to school?'; 'What if I get sick on the bus?'; 'What if I forget my homework?'
Social Anxiety Disorder	Worry about being thought of badly by others, e.g. 'What if I say the wrong thing?'; 'What if they think I'm stupid?'; 'What if they think I'm weird?'; 'What if I can't think of anything to say?'

Avoidance
Avoids separating from parents, e.g. they need a parent in the room to fall asleep, clinginess and distress at school drop-off, refusal to attend play dates or sleepovers.
Avoidance of the feared situation or object, or high anxiety and distress if/when exposure occurs, e.g. refusing to go to a birthday party to avoid contact with balloons; high distress and tantrums in anticipation of a visit to the doctor.
Avoidant behaviours that relate to specific worries, e.g. spending excessive time on homework to avoid making mistakes; reassurance-seeking, e.g. repeatedly checking on the health of a family member or repeatedly asking questions about plans of the next day, to avoid feelings of uncertainty; permissiveness to avoiding conflict with friends.
Avoidance of social situations, especially those where there's a risk of evaluation by others, e.g. refusing to participate in class talks and other public speaking tasks; avoiding any social situations involving new people or larger groups of people; avoiding asking for help and/ or expressing opinions.

How do I know if my child is anxious?

All anxious kids worry about worst-case scenarios and go out of their way to avoid anxiety-provoking situations, but what they worry about and which situations they avoid differs according to their specific type of anxiety. Take Claudia and Oliver below. Claudia is twelve years old and presents with Generalized Anxiety Disorder.

66 She worries about absolutely everything. Last week she got herself into a state because she'd made a minor spelling mistake in class the week before, and convinced herself she'd get in trouble if her homework wasn't perfect. There's no way that would happen because her teacher is really lovely, but I had to check her homework *three times* before she'd calm down, and I could tell she was still worried about it even after that.

She worries about *everything*: getting sick, being on time for school (even though we're never late) and she always has to know exactly what we're doing and when, and loses it completely if plans change.

A few weeks ago, she saw a story on the news about a child who'd been abducted and since then she's pestered us with questions about the house — how safe it is and whether everything's locked — and she's been refusing to get the bus to school with friends even though she'd been doing it for months without any issue. We've tried to reassure her but it makes no difference.

She still sleeps with a nightlight because she's afraid of the dark, and we have to lie with her until she falls asleep or she can't sleep.

It's like as soon as she lies down her head kicks into gear and all of her worries come to the surface. Some nights she doesn't fall asleep before midnight even though we have her in bed by 8 p.m. She's forever complaining that she's got a stomach ache at bedtime, but we know there's nothing wrong because we've been to our doctor about this more than once, and she's told us there's no issue.

Claudia gets so worked up over small things and nothing we do seems to help. I guess we thought she'd outgrow her worry, but she hasn't, and if anything, it's getting worse.

Claudia's anxiety is generalized and she worries about a number of things, but Oliver's anxiety is more specific.

66   Oliver is seven now. He's doing really well at school and has lots of friends, but he has this fear of elevators and balloons that we can't seem to shake. It sounds silly, but he's petrified of both. He's compliant and a well-behaved kid usually, but if he has to go in an elevator or near a balloon, everything changes — he loses it.

We avoid lifts and balloons on purpose where we can, it's just easier, but sometimes that doesn't work. We were shopping last week and everything was fine, but then one of the shops had balloons on display to celebrate a sale, and Ollie lost it. He was inconsolable and completely out of control. When I tried to leave, the quickest way to exit the building was via the lift to the carpark, but there's no way Ollie would have gone for that, so we had to walk to the opposite end of the building to the escalators. I managed to get him out of there eventually, kicking and screaming, but he's refused to go back.

Some of our friends have asked us whether he's acting out for attention, but we really don't think he is. He seems genuinely worried about getting stuck in an elevator and not being able to get out. When he was five we did get stuck in an elevator for about five minutes, but it wasn't a big deal. Maybe that's what started this, though? Balloons we're less clear on. From what we can tell it's the sound of balloons popping that he doesn't like, and the chance he'll be caught off-guard by one popping. Other than that, we can't make sense of it.

Their symptoms are different, but Claudia and Oliver both have anxiety. They each worry about different things and have different patterns of avoidance, but the anxiety they experience is the same, regardless of the cause.

Common symptoms of anxiety in children

If anxiety is a problem for your child, they might:

- seek reassurance about things they're worried about
- ask lots of 'What if ...' questions (e.g. 'What if you're late picking me up?')

- worry about things other kids don't seem to worry about
- worry about things that are highly unlikely and/or a long way in the future
- worry about getting things right and doing things the right way
- focus on worst-case scenarios
- ask for lots of help, more than other kids their age, and/or for tasks they can or should be able to do themselves
- be more sensitive than other kids
- show signs of distress (tears, tantrums) or clinginess on a regular basis and/or in anticipation of the same types of situations
- have trouble sleeping
- refuse to go to bed unless an adult is in the room
- have nightmares on a regular basis
- experience regular stomach aches or headaches (especially first thing in the morning or at night)
- get upset more easily than other kids their age
- want to avoid situations they're worried about
- be slower to warm up to new people or new situations
- avoid trying new things or give up easily (and become upset) when trying new things.

Why do kids develop anxiety?

There's still a lot we don't know about childhood anxiety disorders, but solid research in the last 30 or so years has gone a long way towards bridging our knowledge gap. We now have a much clearer picture, for example, of the factors that increase a child's risk for anxiety, one of the strongest being temperament. An extensive body of research shows that children with an inhibited temperament — children who, from birth, are wary of, and slower to warm up to unfamiliar situations and new people — are more likely to develop an anxiety disorder than children born with other temperaments. Likewise, children with anxious parents are at higher risk for anxiety than children of non-anxious parents, in part due to genetic factors, but also probably other factors like parent modelling.[5] Take research by Professor Andy Field, from the University of Sussex, for example, who set out to examine how parent sharing of fear information might contribute to anxiousness in children. He and his team did this by asking parents to share fear-based, positive, or no information about novel creatures or animals (so that children had no prior knowledge that might bias their views at testing) before testing children's fear beliefs. Their results were interesting. They found that when children were given fear-based information about novel creatures or animals, they developed fear beliefs about that specific creature or animal, but when they were given positive information or no information about the creature/animal, they didn't.[6,7] Even more interesting, this effect was found only when fear-based information was provided by parents. When a peer delivered the same fear-based information, children's fear beliefs didn't change.[8]

Compelling evidence for the role of parent modelling in the development of anxiety disorders also comes from research conducted by Dr Marcy Burstein and Professor Golda Ginsburg at Johns Hopkins University.[9] In their study, parents were trained to act anxiously in one condition, and calm and confident in another, about a planned spelling test their child was to participate in. Compared to when parents modelled calm, confident behaviour, when parents modelled anxious behaviours, children reported higher levels of anxiety, more anxious thoughts and a stronger desire to avoid the planned spelling test. What's interesting about this, is that it seems to suggest that parent modelling can increase a child's experience of anxiety, but also their risk for anxiety by influencing their thinking habits and coping styles, too.

Separate from parent modelling, specific styles of parenting have also consistently been linked to childhood anxiety disorders. Research shows, for example, that parents of anxious children tend to be more overprotective and overinvolved than parents of non-anxious children. The impact of overprotective/overinvolved parenting is twofold: it reinforces and strengthens anxious symptoms by promoting avoidance, and it blocks kids from developing confidence in their ability to cope.[10] Whether this relationship exists because overprotective parenting causes childhood anxiety disorders or is a consequence of child anxiousness is still up for debate, but initial research at least suggests that parents of anxious children are overprotective because their child's anxious behaviour prompts this style of parenting, not because parents of anxious children are overprotective in general without cause.[11]

The above research tells us that both genetic and environmental factors play a role in the development of anxiety disorders. Parent modelling of fear and threat-based information likely plays a considerable role, as do certain styles of parenting, especially those which are overprotective or overinvolved.

If you've parented your child in a way that's contributed to their anxiety, know this: you're not a bad parent. You've parented with your child's best interests at heart, and your over-protectiveness has likely been a reaction to your child's anxiousness, not the cause of their anxiety per se. And regardless of what got your child to this point, it's what you do next that matters most. It's never too late to turn things around. You can help your child build the skills they need to conqueror their anxiety, and build their resilience against future anxiety at the same time, you just need the right strategies.

Start by avoiding avoidance

Whether it's being away from Mum and Dad, a class speech or a visit to the dentist, your child will want to avoid any situation that makes them feel anxious. The more anxiety provoking the situation, the more desperate they'll be to avoid it, which is why massive meltdowns start when feared situations loom. The extent of your child's anticipatory anxiety will make you wonder if avoidance really is the best course of action. After all, encouraging your child to do something that makes them so upset can't be helpful, right? Wrong.

Avoidance will resolve your child's distress in the short term, but make their anxiety worse overall. Not only will they miss the opportunity to learn that worries aren't trustworthy — because the worst-case scenarios they insist are foregone conclusions actually aren't — they'll be robbed of the chance to see that their worries are wrong about their ability to cope too; they can cope with far more than their worries let on.

The solution to anxiety isn't avoidance, it's bravery. Facing anxiety-provoking situations head-on will make your child more anxious initially, but as he or she learns that worries are gross over-exaggerators, this will start to shift. The more practice your child has facing their fears, the more proof they'll have of just how unreliable their worries are, and slowly but surely their anxiety will taper off. Seeing your child distressed will make it hard to persevere, but remember that in their daily activities your child will continue to experience anxiety whether or not you encourage them to face their fears; only this anxiety will be wasteful anxiety. It'll feel awful and worsen over time, without any real purpose. By encouraging your child to face their fears, you're encouraging productive anxiety. Productive anxiety feels just as awful as the wasteful kind, but it's purposeful. It's anxiety that will help your child to feel less anxious in the future, and that's what makes it worthwhile.

Encourage your child to practise being brave

Encouraging bravery is the best way to help your child beat their anxiety and worry, so each time your child expresses a desire to avoid an anxiety-provoking situation, encourage them to face their fears instead. If encouragement is all your child needs to face their fears head-on, terrific. Offer lots of positive praise after each and every success, and keep on with your practice. If taking a stand against anxiety proves too hard, look at how you can help your child practise being brave in smaller steps.

Exactly how you do this will depend on your child's age and the type and severity of their anxiety, but the bravery plan outlined below based on Kate (ten) and her parents is a pretty good example.

66 Kate has always been an anxious kid. She's never liked being away from us, and she's always slow to warm to new people and new situations. It was a nightmare when she started day care. She cried every morning for eight months, and they still had to pry her off my leg each morning well after that. She was a bit better when she started school, but she still struggled. Even now she hates it if we drop her to school before the bell and she needs us to walk her to her classroom.

We always assumed she'd grow out of it, but if anything, things are getting worse. She used to be okay with us going out to dinner if her usual babysitter was available, but she gets so upset when we go out now it's just not worth it. She'll call every ten minutes and ask us to come home, and we both end up so stressed it's just easier to stay home.

She'll only go to a play date if it's a family friend and we go with her. Her friend had a sleepover birthday party a couple of weekends ago and I could tell Kate really wanted to go, but she convinced herself something bad would happen if she went and worked herself into such a state we ended up cancelling. We want to help her but we don't know how.

Kate's parents are desperate to help Kate to feel happier, but supporting Kate's avoidance of separation to help her avoid distress has unfortunately reinforced not just her anxiety, but her uncertainty in her ability to cope in her parents' absence.

Kate needs help practising separation in small, graduated steps. For example:

- Practise walking to the classroom from the school gate once the bell has gone (Mum/Dad to stay at the school gate until Kate has reached her classroom).

- Practise walking to the classroom from the school gate once the bell has gone (Mum/Dad to leave straight away after saying goodbye to Kate at the gate).

- Practise getting to school ahead of the bell and playing in the playground while Mum/Dad stands at the school gate.

- Practise getting to school five minutes ahead of the bell and saying goodbye to Mum/Dad at the school gate (Kate to play in the playground with friends for the five minutes before class).

- Practise getting to school ten minutes ahead of the bell and saying goodbye to Mum/Dad at the school gate (Kate to play in the playground with friends for the five minutes before class).

- Practise leaving Kate with a babysitter while Mum/Dad go out to lunch for an hour. No phone calls between Mum/Dad and Kate.

- Practise leaving Kate with a babysitter while Mum/Dad go to a movie and lunch. No phone calls between Mum/Dad and Kate.

- Practise leaving Kate with a babysitter while Mum/Dad go out to dinner (Mum/Dad to be home before Kate due to go to bed). No phone calls between Mum/Dad and Kate.

- Practise leaving Kate with a babysitter while Mum/Dad go out to dinner (Mum/Dad to be home after Kate due to go to bed). No phone calls between Mum/Dad and Kate.

- Practise Kate having a play date with a friend for one hour. Mum/Dad to wait outside in the car.

- Practise Kate having a play date with a friend of her choice for one hour. Mum/Dad to leave at drop-off.

- Practise Kate having a play date with a friend of her choice for two hours. Mum/Dad to leave at drop-off.

- Practise Kate having a play date, including dinner at a friend's house. Mum/Dad to leave at drop-off.

- Practise Kate having a sleepover at a friend's house. Mum/Dad to leave at drop-off.

Practising separation will initially increase Kate's anxiety. But as she experiences success, she'll learn that, despite what her worries tell her, when she's away from Mum and Dad 1) nothing bad happens, and 2) she *can* cope. Which is why the very thing Kate wants to avoid — separation — and the thing Kate's parents have been supporting her avoidance of, is actually the very thing that will make her less anxious once and for all.

Getting the most out of your bravery practice

Encouraging your child to say no to their worries is what will ultimately help to lessen their anxiety, but there are some basic rules to follow to get the most out of your bravery practice. For starters, learning of any kind requires repetition, so help your child practise on a regular basis. How regularly you need to practise will depend on your child's age and the severity and duration of their anxiety, but as a general rule, you'll see more progress if you undertake bravery practice at least twice a week. Weekly practice is good too, but you'll see faster results with more frequent practice. And if you can only commit to monthly practice or practice every two to three weeks, that's okay, every bit helps, but be patient. Progress with infrequent practice will be significantly slower.

Make sure your practice is graded. Start with easier tasks first before gradually working up to more challenging practices. In the case of Kate, walking to the classroom from the school gate once the bell has gone — with Mum/Dad staying at the school gate until Kate has reached her classroom — is easier to practise than Kate getting to school ahead of the bell, saying goodbye to Mum/Dad at the gate, and playing in the playground until it's time for class. So Kate and her parents need to practise this step repeatedly first, until Kate's anxiety lessens, and then they can move on to practising the next easiest task.

Starting with easier tasks first will help build your child's confidence, and, as they learn that their worries aren't as trustworthy or reputable as they first thought, more challenging tasks will feel less overwhelming.

Introducing bravery practice to your child

You might understand that bravery practice is the key to your child beating their anxiety, but convincing your child to face their fears will be a challenge in and of itself. Your child might want to feel less anxious, but not by feeling more anxious first, and that's where you'll run into trouble. If your child's around six or older, try offering a child-friendly rationale for bravery practice:

> 66 I know that certain things like play dates and sleepovers make you feel worried and anxious, which is why you usually opt to stay home. But I also know you don't like missing out on time with friends, so I've been doing a bit of research about how we can make things better. What I've learnt is that even though staying home makes you feel better at the time, when we let worry and anxiety boss us around, the worry and anxiety get bigger and stronger. When we stand up to the worry and refuse to do what it says, we get bigger and stronger and the worry and anxiety start to go away.
>
> We're going to make a list of all the ways your worry and anxiety tries to boss you around — things like, 'I can't go to sleepovers' — and then we're going to work together to figure out how to boss the anxiety back by not doing what it says. It might mean having to be brave sometimes, because refusing to do what the worry wants you to do can be hard, but I know you can do this, and I'm here to help.

Once you've listed your child's anxious behaviours, including reassurance-seeking behaviours like asking lots of questions, and avoidance behaviours like refusing to ride in elevators, brainstorm ideas for how your child can practise being brave in small steps. The more ideas you have the better, so make your list as comprehensive as you can, and make sure you have at least a few relatively easy tasks for your child to start on. If you're doing your best to brainstorm but can't think where to begin, a few ideas are listed below. The more specific your practice is to your child's anxiety, the better, so try to use these ideas as a guide only.

Area of anxiety: separation at bedtime

Common avoidance behaviours: delay tactics at bedtime; unable to fall asleep without an adult; repeatedly leaving bed after lights out.

Bravery practice:

- Practise falling asleep with an adult in the room, but not in the bed (e.g. on a chair a little away from the bed).

- Practise falling asleep with an adult sitting near the bedroom door (no talking or verbal reassurance).

- Practise falling asleep with an adult sitting outside the bedroom door (no talking or verbal reassurance).

- Practise falling asleep with an adult returning at five- to ten-minute intervals (no talking or verbal reassurance).

- Practise falling asleep with an adult returning at ten- to twenty-minute intervals (no talking or verbal reassurance).

- Practise separating at other times (e.g. staying with a babysitter while Mum and Dad go out).

Area of anxiety: balloon phobia

Common avoidance behaviour: avoid any situations where balloons might be present.

Bravery practice:

- Practise holding a deflated balloon.

- Practise watching YouTube videos of balloons popping and not popping (no sound).

- Practise watching YouTube videos of balloons popping and not popping (sound on low).

- Practise being in the same room as a slightly blown up balloon.

- Practise being in the same room as a balloon blown up to a medium size.

- Practise playing games with a balloon (e.g. trying to keep the balloon off the ground).

- Practise being in the same vicinity (but at a distance) as a balloon as it's popped.

- Practise popping balloons.

Area of anxiety: phobia of dentists

Common avoidance behaviour: refusal to go to the dentist (often expressed through massive tantrums).

Bravery practice:

- Practise reading books about going to the dentist.

- Practise looking at pictures of dentists and dental rooms (cartoon pictures initially, then photos).

- Practise visiting your local dentist and sitting in the waiting room only (no appointment or contact with the dentist).

- Practise role playing dentist visits at home (Mum or Dad pretend to be the dentist and examine teeth).

- Practise attending a dentist visit, no intervention (the goal of this visit is to feel comfortable sitting in the dentist's chair).

- Practise sitting in a dentist chair while the dentist explains what each implement does.

- Practise attending a dentist visit with minimal intervention (dentist to examine teeth visually and without using implements).

Area of avoidance: saying no and/or asking for help

Common avoidance behaviours: avoids asking for help when needs it; says yes to others to avoid saying no.

Bravery practice:

- Practise saying no to siblings when they ask for favours.

- Practise asking a question about a menu item at a restaurant.

- Practise asking the teacher a question in class (privately).

- Practise asking the teacher a question by raising a hand in class.

- Practise saying no to friends.

- Practise asking others for a play date (instead of relying on parents to coordinate).

Convincing your child to practise

Bravery practice means your child has to face their fears, and that's not hugely appealing. Even if your child initially likes the idea of practising being brave, odds are that'll change, so don't rest on your laurels. The idea of feeling more anxious now to feel less anxious later might make perfect sense to you, but as far as your child's concerned, how they'll feel in a week, month or year isn't all that important. How they feel right now is of far greater significance, so if you want your child to feel anxious in the here and now, you're going to have to sweeten the deal. That's where rewards come in.

For your child to consider deliberately bearing the brunt of their anxiety, the rewards on offer will have to be meaningful, so ask what they would like. Let your child know that you know being brave is hard, which is why you want to honour their efforts. Together, list five to ten small rewards, five to ten medium sized rewards, and five to ten big rewards. Toys, video games and other electronics are always popular choices, though rewards don't have to be money based. Things like special time with Mum or Dad, a sleepover with a friend, or time doing a favourite activity are great rewards as well.

If you're unsure about any of your child's suggestions, speak up. Agreeing to a reward now and reneging on it later will undermine the strategy, so make sure you're happy with each reward on your child's list. And if you think some of your child's ideas are a little bit cheeky, give serious consideration to their requests before you say no. Outlandish suggestions like a new computer or iPad are obviously out of the question, but if you're reluctant to say yes to a reward purely because it's outside what you'd usually agree to (e.g. a mid-week dessert or play date) think twice. If your child's anxiety is severe enough to warrant intervention, being brave will be a real test. To be effective, rewards will need to be big enough to counterbalance your child's urge to avoid, so think on that before making any final decisions. (For more on rewards, see 'Introduce rewards' on p. 23.)

If bravery practice isn't working

If you've tried rewards and you still can't convince your child to practise being brave, there are a few other things you can try. First, review your rewards list. If they're not things your child wants, they won't work. Look at what you can change to make rewards more appealing, and start again. If that doesn't work, look at the frequency of your practice. If you think you're practising regularly enough, but you're not making progress, consider more frequent practice. And if you're having trouble getting started or your progress has plateaued, look at your grading. Your child might need a more gradual program than the one you have now, so look at how you can break practice down into even smaller steps. And if you're still having trouble, look at what else your child might need to support their practice. If they have lagging emotion regulation skills and can't tolerate any kind of distress, the skills covered in Chapter 2 are a good place to start; and if your child's a little bit older, the cognitive skills covered below should help as well. Cover off skills-building in other areas first, and come back to bravery practice later.

Help your child break their reassurance-seeking habit

Avoiding triggering situations will make your child's anxiety worse, but so will reassurance-seeking. Answering questions, like 'What if I can't find my friends when I get to school?', 'What if I've forgotten something?', 'What if I can't get to sleep?' or 'What if you're late picking me up?' might help your child feel better in the short term, but it'll also make them feel like they can't cope without you, and that will ultimately make things worse. The more uncertain your child is in their ability to cope, the more they'll worry, and not only will their need for reassurance be greater, their overall anxiety will be stronger as well.

If your child relies on your reassurance to cope with their anxiety, help them break this cycle. Start by explaining how your new approach will work.

" You know how when we do what the worry tells us to do, it makes anxiety worse? Well I think one of the things your worry tells you to do is to ask worry questions. A lot of the questions you ask aren't worry questions, like 'What's for dinner?' but some of them are, like 'What time do we have to leave for school?' I know it's a worry question when I know you know the answer, or when you've already asked me the same question lots of times before.

I've always answered your questions because I thought that was the best way to help, but now I know that when I answer worry questions, the worry wins. It gets bigger and stronger, and you get more anxious, and that's not what I want. So from now on, when you ask me a question that I know is a worry question I'm going to say something like, 'I've answered that question for you before, what did I say last time you asked me?' And then even if you get really upset and want me to answer the question again, I won't, because I don't want the worry to win. Instead, I'll say something like, 'I'm sorry you're so upset, but remember I can't answer worry questions because I'm not going to let the worry win.' I'm on your side and I want you to be happy, so that means not letting the worry boss us around.

Once your child understands how things will work, implement your plan. Understanding a plan in theory and experiencing it are two different things, so know that your child might become distressed when you won't answer their worry questions, no matter how many times you've covered the above rationale. If they do, stick to your plan. Remember, answering your child's questions won't make them less anxious; the more dependent they are on you for reassurance, the more anxious they'll be. It can be hard to stick to your guns when your child's upset, but watching them struggle with anxiety throughout their childhood will be harder. Try a new approach and see where it gets you.

If your child really can't cope with a cold turkey approach, try gradually reducing reassurance-seeking with tokens. Monitor their reassurance-seeking behaviour for a few days to determine their daily baseline (i.e. the number of times they seek reassurance with worry questions/the number of days of monitoring), then issue your child with an equivalent number of tokens. Each time they want a worry question answered, ask them to hand over a token. Once all their tokens are gone, that's it, no more answers. Don't ignore your child just because they're out of tokens; instead, say something like, 'Remember, I can't answer any more worry questions because you've used your tokens for today.' Warn your child when they're running low ('By my count you only have two more tokens to use today') and encourage them to limit their token use where you can ('You only have five tokens; are you sure you want to use one on this question?'). But otherwise let token use be guided by your child. Every three or four days, reduce the token allowance by one or two tokens, until their reassurance-seeking has stopped and the tokens can be packed away. When your child's able to tolerate reassurance-seeking boundaries, offer lots of praise, and if seeking reassurance has been an issue for some time, consider throwing rewards into the mix.

Show your child that their worries lie

Worries lie. They make worst-case scenarios seem far more likely than they really are, and they trick your child into thinking they can't cope when they actually can. They're incredibly persuasive, especially when they join forces with anxiety, which is why it's so hard for your child to ignore them.

But worries only have power so long as they're believable. Right now, your child believes their worries because they don't know any better. That's where you come in. If your child's old enough (around seven years old) and has insight into their worry, you can help them learn skills to test their worries' credibility.

Ask your child to tell you how many times they've had the worry they're having now, before. If it's a longstanding worry, come to a rough weekly estimate, then multiply this by the number of weeks since the worry first started, trying to be as accurate as you can to make your maths more convincing. Once you've got a number, ask your child to think about how many times this particular worry has come true — not a little bit or partially true, completely and irrefutably true. Then divide that number by your worry estimate to get an accuracy rating for your worry. Odds are, it's zero, or close to it, because worries hardly ever come true. Even when they do, the outcome's almost never as catastrophic as initially thought.

If your child has multiple worries, repeat this process and keep a record of each worry's accuracy rating. Then, when the worry pops up next, help your child to remember that each and every time they've worried about this before, they've felt worried for no reason, because the outcome they were worried about never actually happened.

If your child comes back with 'But what if this time it's different and it *does* happen?' don't rely on reassurance: start a worry log. Help your child record their worry prediction — whatever outcome their worry is trying to convince them of — and once the worry period has past, come back to review the outcome to determine whether this time was actually different, or whether the worry lied again, just like it's always done in the past. Do the same thing each time a worry arises, until you have a long list of evidence supporting the fact that your child's worries don't just sometimes lie, they *always* lie.

To really reinforce your point, ask your child how they'd feel if they caught a good friend lying to them. They might be willing to forgive and forget in the first instance if their friend apologized, which is fair enough; but then ask how they'd feel if they caught their friend lying not just a second time, but a third, fourth and fifth time. They probably wouldn't be as willing to forgive, and they may even tell you that they'd stop being friends with that person, or at least stop trusting them. That's when you need to ask why they're so willing to keep on trusting their worries when they've lied to them hundreds of times or more.

Help your child fact-check their worries

For lots of kids, seeing how often their worries lie is a game changer. If they're still having trouble tuning their worry out, help them keep their worry in check with a fact check, just like Sam and his dad.

66   Dad: Okay, so you can't get to sleep because you're worried someone's going to break into the house.

Sam: Yeah.

Dad: These worries are really annoying aren't they? Remember, worries like to lie so let's look at the facts and figure out whether this is one of those times when the worries are trying to trick you into feeling worried when you don't need to be. Has anyone broken into our house before?

Sam: Well, no. I don't think so, have they?

Dad: No, definitely not. We've lived here for fifteen years and we've never had anyone break into the house. Come to think of it, I don't think there's ever been a break-in anywhere in this area. We live in a very safe place. Do you know anyone who's had their house broken into?

Sam: No, but I saw something on the news last week. A man got hurt when someone broke into his house.

Dad: That's really awful. People's houses can get broken into, but that doesn't mean it'll happen to us. What do Mum and I do every night before we go to bed and every day before we leave the house?

Sam: Lock the doors.

Dad: That's right, and we check that all the windows are locked too, so it's impossible for anyone to break in. Our house is completely safe. How often do you worry about this?

Sam: Pretty much every night.

Dad: That's what I thought. And when did you start worrying about it? Is it a new worry or one you've had for a while?

Sam: I've had it for a while. A year? Maybe two. A really long time.

Dad: Okay, so let's say it's been a year, even though it's probably been longer. There's 365 days in a year, which means you've worried about this at least 365 times. Any how many times has it come true? How many times has someone broken into our house?

Sam: None.

Dad: None. Exactly. So, the worries have told you 365 times that our house would get broken into, and it's never happened. Not even once. What do you think about that?

Sam: The worries are lying again.

Dad: Yep. They're pretty tricky, aren't they?

Sam: And really annoying.

Dad: And really annoying. So, what are you going to say to your worries when they try to get you to believe them on this one?

Sam: Get lost worries. You're lying again. My dad and I checked.

Dad: Good job.

Exactly which facts you use to challenge your child's worry will depend on their worry, but good general questions include:

- Have you had this worry before? What happened last time you had this worry? Did the worry come true or did something else happen?

- Your worry is making you focus on one particular outcome, but what else might happen?

- Do other people worry about this? Why don't other people have this worry?

- What would you say to a friend who was worried about this? How would you help them to feel better?

If you're having trouble thinking of what questions to ask, think about why you know your child doesn't need to worry about whatever it is they're worried about, and use that information to prompt their fact checking. You don't need a long list of facts, just a few that are hard to argue against. It'll take hearing these facts more than once to make an impact, so once you've got a few key facts, write them on palm cards and review these with your child any time their worry ramps up.

Help your child solve solvable worries

Worry will make your child so problem-focused they'll forget to think about solutions, and that's where you come in. Not all your child's worries will be solvable, but many will be, so problem-solving is a great skill to develop. Start by taking steps to better understand your child's worry. Their anxiety might make it hard for them to answer general questions, like 'Why are you anxious?' so try to ask more targeted questions to help you pinpoint specific worries: 'It sounds like you don't want to go to school tomorrow. What will your day look like tomorrow? How will tomorrow be different or the same as today?'

Once you understand why your child's feeling anxious, if their worry is a solvable one, help them practise problem-solving skills. Start by asking them to brainstorm a list of possible solutions, good and bad, resisting the urge to jump in with your own ideas if they're slow to start. Solving your child's problems for them might reduce their anxiety now, but it won't help them learn to independently manage their worry, which is your ultimate goal. If solution-focused thinking is a real struggle for your child, step in with a few solutions of your own to get the ball rolling, but make sure you give your child the chance to think for themselves first, and only step in as a last resort. (Younger kids are the exception. They'll have a hard time generating their own solutions, so put two or three of your own ideas forward upfront, making sure your solutions are realistic and age-appropriate.)

Once you have some ideas on the board, help your child decide which solution will best solve their problem. For younger kids, this will be a relatively easy task since both solutions are workable ones suggested by you. If your child's a little older, help them evaluate their solutions list by going through the potential pros and cons of each. Once they've weighed up their options and decided on a course of action, help them consider any relevant practicalities: do they need anyone's help to implement their plan, for example, or is there anything they need in place ahead of time? Then implement their plan. If things go smoothly and the solution resolves your child's worry, great; but if it doesn't, look at how to tweak the original solution to make it work, or move on to solution number two.

Your child will need lots of problem-solving practice before a solution-focused response to worry becomes their new default, so be prepared to put in the hard yards before you see results. Once your child learns that their worries aren't as insurmountable as they initially seem, their anxiety will decrease, and that'll make your efforts worth it.

A few last points on strategy practice

To get the most out of the strategies in this chapter, there are a few key rules you need to follow. First, be dedicated in your approach. If you encourage bravery practice or fact-checking only sporadically, progress won't be nearly as fast as if you help your child practise these skills regularly. So, time your introduction of strategies well. If you know you have a busy month ahead, wait. You're better off delaying the introduction of strategies until you can make practice a priority.

You'll also need to be strategic about the order in which you introduce strategies. If your child's anxiety is relatively mild, they might cope well with behavioural strategies from the outset (e.g. bravery practice, reducing reassurance-seeking). But if their anxiety is more severe, they might need help to learn additional skills first before they can tolerate their anxiety well enough to start behaviour-based strategies like this (e.g. emotion regulation skills like those covered in Chapter 2 or cognitive skills like problem-solving and fact-checking outlined earlier). Which order you introduce strategies will also depend on your child's age. If they can identify what they're worried about and why they're feeling anxious, cognitive skills like problem-solving and fact-checking will work well; but if they can't identify why they're feeling anxious (which is common in younger kids) cognitive strategies won't work and behavioural strategies will be your best bet. Start by encouraging bravery practice and skills for managing distress (see Chapter 2) and, once your child's a little older, introduce additional cognitive strategies if anxiety is still an issue.

And lastly, be patient. Cognitive strategies in particular are hard to learn — even adults have trouble learning to change their thinking. Be prepared to have to practise fact-checking and problem-solving many times over before you see results. Likewise, one lot of bravery practice won't do the trick; your child needs to practise being brave over and over again before you see change. The strategies outlined above work, but repetition is key, and so is your diligence. You'll get out of strategy practice what you put in, so make sure to help your child practise their new skills often. Your efforts will be worth it. Not only will your child feel less anxious, they'll feel more in control of their worry and more confident as well.

The important bits

+ Childhood anxiety disorders are a real and prevalent issue and early intervention is key.
+ Symptoms will vary depending on the type of anxiety, but worry and avoidance are key symptoms of anxiety disorders.
+ Certain factors increase a child's risk for anxiety, including temperament, genetic factors, parent modelling of anxiety and overprotective parenting.
+ Avoidance will help your child cope now, but it'll make their anxiety worse longer term, so don't encourage avoidant coping.

+ Bravery practice, not avoidance, is key to helping your child overcome their anxiety.
+ Practising being brave will make your child more anxious in the short term, but less anxious longer term.
+ Help your child practise being brave on a regular basis, starting with easier practices first.
+ Use rewards. They'll increase your child's willingness to practise being brave.
+ Like avoidance, reassurance-seeking will make your child's anxiety worse, so help them break their reassurance-seeking habit.
+ If your child's old enough, teach them cognitive skills to fact-check and evaluate the reliability of their worries.
+ Help your child to solve solvable worries.
+ Be patient and help your child practise skills regularly, consistently and frequently.

ONE LAST THING

Parenthood is rough. All kids are challenging sometimes, even the seemingly perfectly behaved, perfectly emotionally regulated, confident, socially skilled ones. If you think you're the only parent feeling incompetent and way out of your depth, I promise you you're not. Common childhood challenges are common for a reason. *All* parents struggle with them, even the 'perfect' parents (the ones who look like they have it all together) and the so-called parenting 'experts', myself included.

The truth is, when it comes to parenting, no one has all the answers, so cut yourself some slack. If your child has behavioural issues, anxiety problems, low confidence or trouble making and keeping friends, it's not a sign of bad parenting; it's a sign your child's going through a developmental rough patch and needs a bit of extra help — your help.

Your child's missing the skills they need to be better behaved, more in control of their emotions, less anxious and more confident (depending where your issues lie) and needs your help to learn the skills they need to change. Instructing your child to act differently or criticizing them when they don't won't get you very far. What your child needs is dedicated skills practice, and because they're limited skills- and maturity-wise, that practice has to be led by you. Not only that, but like it or not, your child learns best through repetition. Practice has to be parent-led and done a hundred times over (give or take) before you see any real results.

Being your child's teacher will feel relentless and exhausting at times, but stick with it. The challenges inundating you now will pass, and with a bit of help, your son or daughter will grow to be well-mannered, even tempered, competent and confident, no matter how unlikely that seems right now. It *will* get easier. I promise. And, in the meantime, try not to get so distracted by how much better you think you 'should' be as a parent that you forget you're already a great one — because you are.

ENDNOTES

Chapter 1

1. Wiebe, S., Sheffield, T., Nelson, J.M. et al., 2011, 'The structure of executive function in 3-year-olds', *Journal of Experimental Child Psychology*, 108(3), pp. 436–52.

2. Huizinga, M., Dolan, C.V. and Van der Molen, M.W., 2006, 'Age-related change in executive function: Developmental trends and a latent variable analysis', *Neuropsychologia*, 44, pp. 2017–36.

3. ibid.

Chapter 2

1. Gee, D.G., Humphreys, K.L., Flannery, J. et al., 2013, 'A developmental shift from positive to negative connectivity in human amygdala–prefrontal circuitry', *Journal of Neuroscience*, 33(10), pp. 4584–93.

Chapter 3

1. Cross, D., Shaw, T., Hearn, L. et al., 2009, 'Australian Covert Bullying Prevalence Study (ACBPS)', Child Health Promotion Research Centre, Edith Cowan University, Perth.

Chapter 6

1. Rapee, R.M., Schniering, C.A. and Hudson, J.L., 2009, 'Anxiety disorders during childhood and adolescence: Origins and treatment', *Annual Review of Clinical Psychology*, 5, pp. 311–41.

2. Lawrence, D., Johnson, S., Hafekost, J. et al., 2015, 'The mental health of children and adolescents. Report on the second Australian Child and Adolescent Survey of Mental Health and Wellbeing', Department of Health, Canberra.

3. Bitsko, R.H., Holbrook, J.R., Ghandour, R.M. et al., 2018, 'Epidemiology and impact of health care provider-diagnosed anxiety and depression among US children', *Journal of Developmental & Behavioral Pediatrics*, 39(5), pp. 395–403.

4. Information taken from a table in Beesdo, K., Knappe, S. and Pine, D.S., 2009, 'Anxiety and anxiety disorders in children and adolescents: Developmental issues and implications for DSM-V', *Psychiatric Clinics of North America*, 32(3), pp. 483–524.

5. Gregory, A.M. and Eley, T.C., 2007, 'Genetic influences on anxiety in children: What we've learned and where we're heading', *Clinical Child and Family Psychology Review*, 10(3), pp 199–212.

6. Field, A.P., Argyris, N.G. and Knowles, K.A., 2001, 'Who's afraid of the big bad wolf: A prospective paradigm to test Rachman's indirect pathways in children', *Behaviour Research and Therapy*, 39, pp. 1259–76.

7. Field, A.P., 2002, '"And don't talk to any strange animals": Do we teach children to be phobic?', British Psychological Society Annual Conference, Blackpool, in Field, A.P. and Lawson, J., 2003, 'Fear information and the development of fears during childhood: Effects on implicit fear responses and behavioural avoidance', *Behaviour Research and Therapy*, 41, pp. 1277–93.

8. Field, A.P., Argyris, N.G. and Knowles, K.A., 2001.

9. Burstein, M. and Ginsburg, G.S., 2010, 'The effect of parental modeling of anxious behaviors and cognitions in school-aged children: An experimental pilot study', *Behaviour Research and Therapy*, 48(6), pp. 506–15.

10. Hudson, J.L. and Rapee, R.M., 2004, 'From anxious temperament to disorder: An etiological model of generalized anxiety disorder', in R.G. Heimberg, C.L. Turk and D.S. Mennin (eds), *Generalized Anxiety Disorder: Advances in research and practice*. New York: Guilford Publications Inc., pp. 51–76.

11. Hudson, J.L., Doyle, A.M. and Garr, N., 2009, 'Child and maternal influence on parenting behavior in clinically anxious children, *Journal of Clinical Child & Adolescent Psychology*, 38(2), pp. 256–62.

INDEX